Recipes from the Wagstaff Miscellany

Edited by

Daniel Myers

CONTENTS

INTRODUCTION

The book known as the Wagstaff Miscellany, or Beinecke MS 163, is a collection of handwritten manuscripts in Latin and Middle English, containing entries on a wide range of subjects. It is currently held at Yale University's Beinecke Rare Book and Manuscript Library.

The manuscript was probably gathered together in the late fifteenth century by John Whittocksmead, an English gentleman and member of Parliament. The 189 recipes in the Wagstaff miscellany are on pages 56r through 76v, which is a portion of the manuscript dated to around 1460.

Images of the original manuscript are freely available on the Yale University Library website. The recipes have previuously been transcribed and edited by Constance B. Hieatt and published as *An Ordinance of Pottage* (London, Prospect Books, 1988), however that edition is no longer in print.

My goal in creating this transcription was to make the recipes widely available to food historians in a usable form. I have done my best to provide an accurate, but readable transcription. Common abbreviations have been expanded, the letters thorn and yogh have been replaced with their modern equivalents, and some minor punctuation has been added.

THE TEXT

[the recipes begin on f.56r]

Here bygynnyth the chapters of diuers makyng and dytyng of potages and flesch sodyn & rostyd and of sleying and dyghtyng of wylde fowle and of makyng of dyvers sotyltys, wortys, in lentyntyme other in fleschtyme.

[left column]

Canebens
Canebens with bacon
Buttyrd wortys
Caboches
Hare other gose powdryde in wortys
Jowtys in flesch tyme
Lentyn foyles
Blaunche porre
Pome porre
Gyngaudre
Elys in sorey
Pykys other elys in ballocbroth
Frumente in lentyn wyth porpoys
Pylets in farcene
To make iussall
To make leche lardes of iij colours
To make iumbelys of a dere
Greuell enforsed

3

Gawdon of Salmon
Cokkes of byllyng
Leche pernen
Feletys in galentyn
Humbelys of purpoys or of other fysch
Numbelys if venson
Purpays in galentyn
Purpays or vensone in brothe
Hare in cyve
Hare in papuld
Hare in talbut
Conynge in grave
Conyngys in syve
Conyngys in clere brothe
Oisters in grave
Oisters in cyve
Chekens in gretney
Creteyney
Capons in conseps

[right column]

Chekens in caudell
Sowpes
Chawdon of veell
Chawdon of pyggys fete
Dowce desyre
Breuet of Lombardy
Bruet of Almyne
Bruet of Spayne
Bruet roos
Chykenes in bruett
Stewe Lombard
Stewyde colops
Brewett Tuskyn
Brewet Sarcenes
Bruet of kydes
Blanche bruety
Sauce sarceney
Eell in butryade

4

Pynonad
Kyde stued
Stuede pertyrygge
A losede beef
Pyke in sauce
Turbut rostyde in sauce
Salmone rostyde in sauce
Brawne in confyte
Blaunchede branie
Leche lumbard
Tayle
Blaunchede sorre
Blaw maungere
Chykeney
Blanke desyre
Sage
Sipres
Florey
Crem boyled
Lyede milke
Mortruys of flesch
Mortrus of fysch

[f.56v]

[left column]

Blaunche mortruys of fysch
Blaunche mortruys of flesch
Payne fondew
Caudell
Caudell ffery
Charlett
Perys in confite
Pesys in composte
Perys in syryppe
Brawne ryall braune sypres brawn bruse
Brawn ryall
Betreyn in lentyn
Betreyn in fleyschtyme

5

Storgon for sopers
Cold lech viaund
Leche lumbard
Cold bruet of rabets
Diuers desyre
Viauntes ryall
Maumene ryall
Gely of fysch dayes
Cristell gely
Gely of fleysche
Crem of almondys
Hages of almayne
Quistes
Joutes
Rastons
Samarcays
Longe fretours
Payne purdyeu
Peletes of porke in dores
Hattes
In lentyn
Sauce madam
Sauce camelene for quaylys
And other manner of fowlys & for fysche
Caudone of swane or of wylde gose
Wellyde pepyre for rostyde well
Fresche lamprey baton
Farteys of fleysch
Fartlettees
Bakyne purpas
Pyes of flesche caponys and fesauntes
Crustade lambard

[right column]

Chauet of beef
Bakyn chikenes
Chauet rial
Chauet of fysche dayes
Porialet

Prennerall
To make posset
Pyes of pares
Brinecy
Losynges opyne
Harbelade opyne
Lesche fryde
Bakyne mete one fysche days
A bakyne mete opyne
A colde bakyne mete
Caudell of almonds
For to sle aner of foules
And reste hem & syne for othure
Crane rostyde
Pertryche rostyde
Quayle rostyde
Heyrone rostyde
Bytore rostyde
Egrott rostyde
Curlew rostyde
Brew rostyde
Conyng rostyde
Rabetes rostyde
Sarcell rostyde
Plouere rostyde
Snyte rostyde
Wodkoc rostyde
Kyd rostyde
Well rostyde
Vensone rostyde
The seydys of a dere
Of his grece
Chikenes farsyde
Chikenes endoryde
Fylets of porke Endoryde
Capons of his grece rostyde
Capons stewede
Pecydaw
Gose or capons farsyde
Pyggys y farsyde

[f.57r]

Pestys of motyn in sause
Dyghtyng of al manner of fysch trowghte boyled
Crab lopster
Breme in sauce
Breme in brothe
Tenche in brothe
Sole in brothe
Sturgeon
Haddoc in gryue
Sowpes chaunlayn
Codlyng lyng haddoc other hake
Base mylet other brem
Congure turbut halibut poiled
Gurnard other roche boyled
Plays soles flounders boyled
Welkes boyled
Perche boyled
Fresch makerell boyled
Schrympes boyled
Sowpys endore
Hote mylke of almonds
Colde mylke of almonds

[1.] (untitled)
Take caules and stryp hem fro the stalkes and betes borage an ane
vyolet malves percely betayn prymrose paciens the wyghthe lekes
croppes of netels perboyle hem & ley hem on a borde presse out
the watyr hewe hem small and do ther to otemele take the broth of
the congure turbut othir good fysche as of salmon do hit in a pott
withe the foresaid herbes when the broth ys at the boylyng caste in
the wortys & the herbes boyle hem up loke they be salte and yf
thou lacke brothe boyle elys take hem up stripp of the fysch from
the bonys grynd hit tempre hit with the selfe broth do al to gedyr in
a pott un to the wortys be forsayd & boyle hem up also then
mayste yf thou wil sethe mustulis sett hem over the fyre and do to
hem as moche watyr as thay may flete yn boyle hem tyll they opyn
then poure oute the broth thorow a streynour pyke the mustulys
grynd hem tempere hem up with the silfe broth and draw hem
thorough a streynour take the same manner of herbes as thu dedist
by fore and the broth of the mustulys sette on the fyre boyle hem
up when the herbes be boyled y nought caste in the mustulys
drowe yn salte and yf thou wylte thou mayste draw pesyn thorow a
streynere and [f.57v] make up the wortys with fayre watyr put ther
yn clere oylle lete them be frydd in by fore the boylyng & lay up
with the forsayde peson and lete none ottemele come ther yn also
thou mayste yf thow will perboyle the white of lekeys and presse
out the watyr hew them smalle take canbenys and fayre watyr &
sett hem on the fyre & when they boyle doyn the white of lekys
loke none ottemele come ther yn salt them & serve them forth.

[2.] For to make canabenes
Take white benes ley hem in watyr rennyng too days and change
the watyr take hem & ley hem dry then dry hem hard uppon a ston
or a pon a este than shylle them atte a tjylle and do a way the
evehys and close the benys iij or iiij at the most and then make hem
clene and so may thou kepe hem as longe as thou wylte.

[3.] Canabens
Take kanbens wesch hem and yf thu wilte stoppe hem a lytyll &
make hem up with mylke of almondys put ther to sugure and salt
out of lentyn make hem up with cowe mylke and put ther to sygure
and salte and buttyrr claryfyde.

9

[4.] Canabens With Bacon
Do suete brothe yn a potte wesche the canabens clene and do ther to and boyle yt up put no lykure ther to loke thay be salte & serve hem take ribbys of bacon boylyd do a way the skyn and ley hem on a dysch and serve hem forther as ye serve venson yn brothe.

[5.] Butturd Wortys
Take al maner of good herbes that thu mayste gete peke hem wesche hem hewe hem boyle hem in fayre watyr put buttyr ther to claryfyyd a grete dell when they be boylyd y now salte hem lete non otemele come ther yn dyse brede too smale gobettys and do yn dyschys and powre there wortys ther upon and serve hem forth.

[6.] Cabogys
Take white cabogys kutt hem fro the stalkes in grete pesys weche hem clene perboyle hem wesch presse out the watyr and hew hem but a lytyll and in flesch tyme do fayre broth of beth or of caponys or of othir good flesch in a potte when hit boylleth do ther to thi cabochis and mary bonys al to brokyn boile hit up do ther to safron and salt when hit ys boyllyd y now alay hit up with gratyd bredde and boylle yt a lytyll and serve hit forth.

[7.] Hare or goose powdryd in wortys
Take good brothe of beef and of othir good flesch & mary bonys do hit in a potte sett hit ovyr the fuyre chop an hare in pecys and do ther to and yf thu wille weshe hym yn the same broth that thu wille boyll hym yn then draw the broth thorow a strayner with all the blod then take caulys & the white of lekys and othyr herbes and ottemele and hew hem small to gedyr and yf hit be an olde hare lete hym boyle well or thu caste yn the wortys yf he [f.58r] be a yonge hare cast hym and thy wortys to gadyr also take a goose of a day and a nyght powdryng chop here & put here in the wortys yn the same maner.

[8.] Joutys yn flesch days
Take kawlys & percelly and othir good herbes perboyle hem welle yn watyr presse out the watyr hew hem ryght smalle or grynd hem and yf thu wylte thu may hew a lytylle fat porke ther wyth and grynd hit ther with and temper hit up with swete porke loke hit be sum delle chaungant of the herbes do yt in a pot boyle & halye hit

up a lytyll ther with and yf thu wylte thou may draw bredde with sum of the brothe then salt hem and serve hem forth with ribbys of bacon or with fat flesch yf thu wylte and one fysch days thu may perboyle herbes & make hem up in the same maner with broth of fresch fysch or elys with thykke mylke of almondys and sigure & salt and lete non othir lykure come there yn.

[9.] Lentyn foyles

Take the same maner of herbes as thu dost to jowtys and onyons clere paryd perboyle hem presse out the watyr do hem yn a potte frye reysons in clere oyle that have be fryed yn byfore and do ther to with a perty of the oyle and boyle hit up with the mylke of almondys and put ther to sugure & salte.

[10.] Longe wortys

Take the same maner of herbes boyle peson take hem fro the fyre take out the cleryst and make hem with the same maner of thyngys save sygure and serve hit.

[11.] Blaunche pore

Take thyke melke of almondys do yt in a potte perboyle the whyte of lekys tendour presse out the watyre hew hem smalle grynd hem temper hem with the same mylke do to gedyr with sygure and salt boyle hit up yf thu wilte thu mayste alay with payndemayn othir with cromys of white brede draw hem with the same mylke and serve hit forth with salte ele yf thu have hit.

[12.] Pome perre

Boyle white pesyn hool hem take hem fro the fyre when they have restyd a whyle then take the cleryst in to a nothir pott then have mylke of almond drawyn up with wyen figes of amely sigure and salte and yf thou wylte reysons fryed w lytyll & do to gedyr boyle hit kepe hit and serve hit forth.

[13.] Gingaudre

Take the hedde of hake fysch the sound and the lever do hit in a pott to gadyr make clene the poke of the sayd hake and do hit ther to sethe hit well in brothe of the selfe fisch or fayre watyr tyll hit be tendour then take yt up lay hit on a bord peke a wey the bondys & safe the fysch hole dyse the lever & the sound yf the poke be not tendour y now sethe hit bettyr and do hit to gedyr kut white brede temper hit with the same brothe and wyne draw hit thorow a lyour put yn [f.58v] a pott put ther to poudyr of pepyr gynger and poudyr of canell and a good colour of sandryn set hit on the fyre ster hit when hit boyleth put hit in the fysch and ster hit esely for brekyng and sesyn hit up with powdyr of gynger and a lytyll venyger & salt then lete hytt no more boyle thu may yf thu wilte take the sound and the lever & the poke of the codlyng and make hit in the same manere.

[14.] Eles yne sorre
Fle eles chop hem yn gobenys do hem yn a potte with onyons and herbes hew hem to gedyr with hole clowys macys powdyr of pepyr powdyr of canell a grete dele & fayre watyr & draw lyour of bredde with wyn do hit to gedyr sett hit on the fyre ster hit when hit ys boyled y now colowr hit up with sawndrys sesyn hit withe poudyr of gynger venyger & salt and lete hit no more boyle.

[15.] Pykes or elys in ballocbroth
Splett pykes scale hem clene & culpon eles small put hem yn a potte put ther to onyons mynsyd grete & herbes sese hem up with a lyour of bredd and put to hem stockefysch put ther to macys & clowys and powdyr of canell y nowe and a lytyll saveryn and put to hem stockfysch a qutte lyk un to and lete the pyke seth in a esy sause & serve hole pykys for lordys & quarters for othir men & culpons loke they be sesynde yn kynde and put broth y now upon the pyke & serve hym forth.

[16.] Frumente yn lentyn
Take clene pykyd whete bray hit yne a morter and fanned clene & seth hit tyl hit be brokyn than grynd blaunch almondys yn a morter draw ther of a mylke do hit to gedyr & boyle hit tyl hit be resonabulle thykke than loke thy whete be tendyr colour hit up with safferyn leche thy purpas when hit ys sodyn than ley hitt on dysches by hit sylfe and serue hit forth withe frumente.

[17.] Pylets yn sarcene
Take fresch porke or motyn sodyn peke out the bonys hew the flesch small & grynd hit smal yn a morter and temper hit with eyron yn the gryndyng putt ther to pepyr safferyn & salt take fresch

broth clene tryed set yt over the fyre in large vessell lete hit boyle
then sesyn hit with the same colour then make smal rounde ballys
put hem yn a boylyn broth & lete hem boyle ther yn tyll they be y
now then take hem up lete hem drye lete thy broth keyl blow of the
fat take almondys wesch hem temper hem up with the same broth
draw ther of a kynd mylke put the mylke in a swete potte set hit on
the fyre put ther to powdyr of pepyr & canell & a pertyon of
sawndrys to colour hit sarcene colour loke thy most colour be of
hys owne kynde put ther yn clowys macys reysons of coraunce lete
hit boyle as thy seyyst that good ys yf hit be tt thike a lay hit with
swete wyne and do ther to sugur when thy spycez [f.59r] beth
tendour put yn peletys in the same broth ghyf hym atarage of
poudyr of pepyr of gynger and vergys & serve forth the pelets with
the bruet iij or iiij yn a dysche as a potage for the secunde course.

[18.] To make Jussall
Take swete broth of capons or elys or broth as thu may have set hit
on the fyre in a brode vessell colour hit with saveryn put sage ther
to out grote and saffron breke eyron styr hem well to the eyron and
to thy herbes be mellyd to gedyr when hit be gynnys to seth take
out thy potstyke and turne ty crud aboute with the scome loke thy
fyre be not to hasty wh whene hit ys thorow knyt take hit of the fyr
and cover hit & serve hit forth.

[19.] To make leche lardys of iij colours
Take clene cow mylke and put hit in iij pottys breke to everych a
queantyte of eyron as thu seist best ys to do rede colour with
saundres & a nothyr with saveryn the iij with grene herbys put to
everych a porcyon of clene larde of fat of bacon well sodyn &
pertyd in iij pottys put to salt boyle hem all at ones stere hem well
for brennyng yn the boylyng take hem downe cast hem in to a
cloth everych a bove other and wynd the cloth to gedyr & presse
out all the juse than take hem out all hole and make leches of hem
and do iij or iiij leches in a dysch and serve hem forth.

[20.] To make umbelys of a dere
Take the umbelys of a dere blod & all perboyle hem in fresch broth
then take hem up stale broune crustys of brede in the same broth
then cut thy umbelys small & put hem in a potte to the same broth
tryyd in a streynour sesyn hym ther with that they be kyndky

rennyng do to pepyr canell & tempyr hit up with swete wyne put hit to the umbelys loke thy colour stond by the canell sesyn hit with salt & serve hit forth.

[21.] Grewel enforsed
Take merybonys & fresch beef make good gruell ther of than draw hem thorow a streyner take fayre porke tender sodyn peke out the bonys & the senowys & do a wey the skyn grynd hit smal yn a morter temper hit up with the same gruell that ys grownd make hit smothe let hit stond resonabely by the flesshe sesyn hit up with salt & saferyn that sette hym by the fyre lete hym boyle a lytyll and serve hym forthe.

[22.] Chaudon of Salmon
Take al the draught of a samon make hit clene as thu may do hit yn a pote [f.59v] and al the blod of a samon ther with boyle that tyl hit be y nowghe yn the broth of the same fysch take hit up hew hit smalle yf hit be a femaule grynde the spaun do hit to gedyr to the broth draw a lyour of white bredde with swete wyne do ther to poudyr of peper & canell sett hit on the fyre stere hit when hit boylez seson hit up with powdyr of gyngyr venyger salt & safferyn thu may serve hit forth yn the stede of potage or els sause of samon.

[23.] Cokkes of kellyng
Take cokkes of kellyng cut hem smalle do hit yn a brothe of fresch fysch or of fresch salmon boyle hem well put to mylke and draw a lyour of bredde to hem with saundres safferyn & sygure and poudyr of pepyr serve hit forth & othyr fysch amonge turbutt pyke samon choppyd & hewyne sesyn hem with venyger & salt.

[24.] Felets yn galentyne
Take the ribbys of a breste of porke fle of the skyn do the flesche on a broche roste hit tyl hit be almost ynowghe take hit of chop hit yn pecys do hit yn a potte with onyons cut grete wyth clowys hole macyz quibibys do to gedyr & a quantyte of swete broth draw a lyour of paryngys of crystys of white bredde with good wyne and a lytyll blod & alaye hit a lytyll & do ther to poudyr of pepyr a lytyll & a good quantyte of poudyr of canell loke that hit be nott chargaunt sesyn hit up with poudyr of gynger & salt venyger & salt.

[25.] Leche proven
Take mylke of almondyes tempyr hit wyth wyn white wyne and take watyr percellye & oynons cut do ther to elys choppyd & boyled do ther yn saferon & hole pepyr & hole clowys seson hit up with powdyr & salt.

[26.] Numbelys of purpas or of other fysche
Perboyle the numbelys of purpays & thu wylte sum of the fysch cut hit smalle do hit yn a pott draw a lyour of crustys with brede wyth the same broth & som what of the blod and red wyn do hit to geder yn a potte with powder of gynger clowys and canell boyll hit stere hit seson hit up with powder of gynger venygger and salt. Make numbelys of codlyng in the same maner and of other gode fyssh also & serve them forthe.

[27.] Purpays yn Galanteyn
Take purpays do a way the skyn cutt hit yn smal lechys no more then fynger or els take bred drawen wyth red wyne put there to powder of canell powdyr of pepyr boil al seson hit up wyth powder of gynger venegre & salt.

[28.] Purpays or Venyson in broth
[f.60r] Take chikenys of purpas and more of the fysch yf thu wylte chopp hit in pecys with onyons & herbes cut grete & hole clowys & macys powdyr of pepyr & canell & do to gedyr in a pott wythe fayre watyr or with broth of the fysch and with a perty of wyne boyle hit up yf the fysch be goode hit wille a lay hit sylfe or els draw a lytyll lyour of crustys & do ther to poudyr of gynger & salt and make venyson in broth in the same maner.

[29.] Hare yn cyve
Smyte a hare in small pecys perboyle hem yn swete broth with hys own blodd cast hym yn a cold watyr peke hym clene do hym yn a pott claryfyd claryfye the broth clene do ther to onyons & herbes mynsyd take hole clowys macys & powdyr & draw ther yn a lyour of crustys with rede wyne boyle hit tyl hit be ynowghe sesyn hit up with powdyr of gynger venyger & salt & loke hit be a good colour of blod.

[30.] Hare yn papald

Take a hare chop hym pecys perboyle hym yn watyr claryfe the broth put to thy flesch boyle hyt seson hit up with douce poudyr & salt take losyngez of past frydd of wafrons cowch hem in a dysches & poudyr the sewe a boyvyn.

[31.] Hare yn talbut

Choppe a hare yn pecys perboyle hym yn good broth with hys owne blode trye the flesch yn a potte grynd almondys unblaunched tempyre hem up with the same brothe & put mylke there to and do therto onyonys perboyld hole spicer and powdyr for the sesyn hit up poudir and salt a quantite of wyne and a lytil sugur.

[32.] Conynggez in grave

Perboile conyngges in gode brothe take them up smyte them in peces make hem clene do hem in a pott with hole clowis macys & onyons y cut somedel grete in pouder blaunche almondys grynd hem & draw up withe the same brothe a thike mylke & do to gedyr suger boyle hit loke hit be salt messe hit forthe cast ther on a dragge of clowys macys a mynsyd gynger and blaunch poudyr.

[33.] Conynggez in Cyve

Chop conyngys in pecys do hem in a pott take onyons and good herbes y choppyd to gedyr boyle hem up in swete brothe do ther to poudyr [f.60v] of pepyr make a lyour of paryngys of crustys of swete bredde drawyn with wyn and a lytle blode alay hit up but a lytyll do ther to poudyr of canele a grete dele sesyn hit up with poudyr of gynger wenggur [vinegar?] & salt.

[34.] Conyngges yne clere broth

Chop conyngys in pecys wesche hem clene do hem yn a pott put ther to clene broth & rede wyne boyle hem till they be y nowghe loke hit nowght much of the broth sesyn hit up with poudyr of gynger a grete quantyte and vergyes and draw hit thorow a streynoure loke hit be salt & serve hit forthe.

[35.] Oysters in grave

Schelle oystrys in to a pott and swette ther with put ther to fayre watyr perboyle hem take hem up put hem yn fayre watyr peke hem clene blaunch almondys grynd hem tempyr heme up with the same

16

broth draw up a good mylke do hit in a pott with onyons and hole spycez and a lytyll poudyr of sygure boyle hit to gedyr & doo the oystres ther to & serve hit forth & caste ther yne youre dragge of hole spicys a bovyn & blaunche poudyr.

[36.] Oystres yn Cyve

Shele oystrys perboyle hem in fayre watyr and the selfe owet & wasch hem yn fayre watyr pyke and trye the broth thorow a streynoure do to gedyr make hem up as thy dyd the conyngys al save the blod & colour hem with saunders.

[37.] Chikens in gretney

Boyle chikens in broth good broth and rese the thyys and the wyngys & the brestys take mylke of almondys unblanched draw up withe the same brothe & poudyr of canell & a perty of wyne sygure saffron & salt do hit to gedyr yn a pott set on the fyre stere hit when hit boyles sesyn hit up with poudyr of gynger & vergeus lay the chikenys hote yn dysches have yolkes of eyron sodyn hard & fryed a lytyll couche on a boute the wyngez & the thyes.

[38.] Creteyney

Take capons and othir fowlys perboile hem dyse hem cast hem yn a pott with cowe mylke & boyle hit ther withe drawe payndmayne withe som of the mylke and put to gedyr take sodyn eyron hew the white & cast ther to sesyn hit up with poudyr sigure & safferyn & salt and a ley hit up with yolkes of eyron sodyn hard & frye hem a lytyll ley hem in disches poure the sewe a bovyn and floresch hit withe anneys in comfite.

[39.] Capons yne conceps

Take capons halfe rostyde do hem yn a pott put ther to swete broth & a perty [f.61r] of rede wyne stew hit up to gedyr that hit be ynowghe trye the brothe yf thu wylte thu may do ther to a lytyll lyoure of payndemayn take eyron sodyn harde hew the white do ther to sigure safron & salt set hit on the fyre when hit boyles a lay hit up withe yolkes of eyron loke hit be rennyng sesyn hit up withe poudyr of gynger & vergeys a rese the thyys & the whyngez & the brestz of the capons loke that they honge by ley hem yn disches plante hem withe hard yolkes of eyron and poudyr & the sewe a bovyn.

[40.] Chikens yne caudell

Take chikens & perboyle hem yn good licoure tyl they be ynowghe coloure the brothe with safron take up the chikens rese the whyngez and the thyys & the brestys a ley up the broth with yolkez of eyron in the maner of a caudell sesyn hit up with sygure & salt couche the chikens yn dishches & dresse the sewe a bovyn & strew on poudyr of gynger & serve hit forthe.

[41.] Soupes

Take marye do hit yn a pot with hony poudyr of pepyr poudyr of gynger canell & a leye hit take brede cut hit yn gobettys tost hem couche hem yn dysches loke thy syryp be salt ghyf hit a colour of safron and serve hit forthe.

[42.] Chaudon of Veel

Take the bowels of veel make hem clene seth them in fresshe brothe cut hem smalle take pouder and wyne or veneger and alay hit with brede take past of flour of whete and make pelettez and them in grece and put to geder.

[43.] Chaudon of Pigges fete

Take swynes fete clene scallyd the groyne and the erys boylid in fresshe brothe take hem up kut them smalle do hit in a potte trye the brothe drawe a thyn lyoure of white brede and wyne and put hit to gedire and make a thyn foyle of past cutt yn smale pelettez frye them seson them up wyth pouder of pepire and safron and salt and do the pelettez hote in dysshes and do the sewe a bove.

[44.] Bonse desire

Take blaunche almondez grynde them drawe them up wyth swete brothe and swete wyne do ther do a quantite of white sugur do hit in a pott and cast ther do take porke wel sodyn tender and grynde hit smalle and medill hit wyth yolkys of eyron pouder and salt and make pelettes ther of [f.61v] the gretnys of the yolke have a bature of yolkes of eyron & paryd floure turne the pelets ther yn take hem frye hem rolle hem up in a panne that they may be round lay ham hote yn dysches dresse the sewe a bovyn loke hit be renyng and on do the fisch dayes thou may withe pike haddok or codlyng do in the same maner.

[45.] Bruet of lumbardy

Take hennys chikens conyngys or othere flesch sodyn do hit in a morter do ther to mylke of almondys do ther in pepyr and alay hit with bredde & do ther in yolkes of eyron sodyn hard growndyn & drawyn up withe percelly & do ther to a lytyll grece or claryfyd boture or the fat of porke & sesyn hit up with poudyr salt & venyger & make hit rede as blod.

[46.] Bruet of Almayn

Take beef or porke chopyd in pecys cast hem yn a pott grynd almondys draw hem with swete brothe & put hit yn the flesch boyle hit & put ther to poudyr of pepyr & sygure when hit ys yboyled y nowghe sesyn hit up with poudyr of gynger & vergeys & coloure hit al rede as blode with.

[47.] Bruet of Spayne

Cut venson yn longe leches & frye hem or rost hem with poudyres weshe hem in wyne take sygure & mylke of almondys clowys macyz and quibibis boyle hit to gedyr & seson hit up with poudyr & venyger.

[48.] Bruet roos

Take the flesch of a roo chop hit perboile hit trye hit and do hit yn a potte take the same broth or othir swete broth draw thorow a streynour & put hit to flesch with onyons ande herbis & hole clowys macys & quibibis & boyle hit & yf be nede alay hit with crustys or els with white brede & with a lytyll of the same broth & of the same blod coloured with safron salt & with poudyr of pepyr & more of canelle & serve hit forth make al othir sewys in the same maner.

[49.] Chikens yn bruet

Take chikens colord & trye the broth in til a pot wyn & sygure do ther to & seson hit up with poudyr of gynger vergeys & canelle that ys drawyn thorowz a streynour & colour hit with saffron.

[50.] Stewe lumbard

Take porke rost hit chop hit and do hit yn a pott & wyn & sygur & hole onyons clowys gynger saffron & saunders & almondys fryyd & temperyz hit up withe poudyr of gynger galentyn & canell

coloure hit with saffron & saunders the chese and other stewyd
lumbardys grynd almondys draw hem up with swete broth take
veele & porke & pare hit clene from the skyn hew hit smalle grynd
hit & medyl hit with mynsyd datys reysons of corans and [f.62r]
and gode powder stere hitt welle when hit boyleth make hitt in
pelettz as grete as a plome sette the mylke on the fyre styre hitt wel
when hitt boylyth cast in the pelettez and lette hit stewe up on the
fyre and do the to powdir and salt and serve hyt forthe.

[51.] Stewy colops
Take colops of venyson rostyd do hem yn a pott do wyn ther to
hole spycez & poudyr of pepyr & canell boyle hit up weth a perty
of swete brothe sesyn hit up with poudyr of gynger & venyger &
serve hit forth.

[52.] Bruet tuskyn
Take broth of capons & of marybonys & of othir goode flesch do
hit yn a pott chop chikenys yn pecys and herbes & hole clowys
macys poudyr of pepur do hit to gedyr set hit on the fyre grynd
porke & wele rawe with yolkes of eyron sodden hard put ther ro
reysons of coraunse poudour& salt & saffron & medyl hit to gedyr
& set hit on the fyre & when youre pott boylez make hit in pelets
as grete as notys cast hem yn the boylyng & coloure hit with juyse
of percelley & of othir good herbes boyle hit up & put ther to a
lytyll good wyne sesyn hit up with poudyr of gynger & venyger &
serve hit forth.

[53.] Bruet sarcenes
Take venyson boyle hit trye hit do hit yn a pott take almond mylke
drawyn up with the same brothe cast ther yn onyons & a ley hit up
withe floure of rye & caste yn cloves aftyr the boylyng take hit don
sensyn hit up with poudyr wyn & sygure & coloure hit with
alekenet.

[54.] Bruet of kedes
Take a kede welle chopyd perboyled & tryed do hit yn a pott take
almondys & do ther to that ys draw up wyth fresche broth do ther
to hole cloves & aley hit up with floure of rye & do ther yn grece
and aftyr the boylyng sesyn hit up with venyger poudyr of pepyr
gynger & canel & sygure & salt & cast ther to.

[55.] Blaunch Bruet
Take hennys or porke rostd & chopyd do hit yn a pott do almonde
[f.62v] mylke ther to aley hit up with floure of rye do ther yn a lytyll
broth & a quantyte of wyne clovys & macys & sesyn hit up with
venyger & pouderes & a lytyll sygure strenyned with alekenet.

[56.] Sauce sarcenes
Make a thykke mylke of almondys do hit in a pot with floure of rye
safrone gynger macys quibibis canel sygure & rynse the bottom of
the disch with fat broth boyle the sewe byfore & messe hit forth.

[57.] Veel in bucnade
Chop vele in pecys do hit in a pot do ther to onyons cut grete &
herbes & good pouderez clovys macyz sygure safron & salt &
boyle hit with a lytyll swete broth than put ther to good cow mylke
boyle hit up with yolkes of eyron lete hit be rennyng & serve hit
forth & make hit with cowe mylke in this maner a fore sayd & thu
mayste make hit with almond mylke in the same maner and when
hit ys boyled sesyn hit up withe poudyr of gynger & vergeys.

[58.] Pynonad
Take mylke of almond drawyn with swete broth do ther to pynes a
grete dele then take wardons quinsys & costardys sodyn &
groundyn and drawyn thorow a streynour withe wyne & good
pouders do to gedyr boyle hit serve hit forth.

[59.] Kyd stewyd
Take a kydde & yf thu will thu may roste hit a lytill or also chop hit
raw in pecys do ther to onyons & herbes & swete broth & wyne
hole clovys macys & othir pouderys & stew hit to gedyr sesyn hit
up with the same gynger or galentyn & with a lytyll lyour of bred
safron & salt & serve hit forth.

[60.] Stewyde pertrych
Take a pertrych or a woodecoke drawyn wasch hem clene chop
hem with hole pepyr couche hem yn a pott of erthe do ther to
datez y cut grete & reysons of corawnce & wyn & as muche of
swete broth & do ther to salt stop the pot set hit on a cole of fyre
when hit ys y boylede y nowghe sesyn hit up with poudyr of gynger
& vergeys & do ther do a lityll colour of safron.

[61.] A losed beef
Take lyr of beef cut hit in lech lay hem a brode on a borde take the fatnes of motyn or of beef herbys & onions hewyn smal to gedyr & strew hit [f.63r] on the leches of beef with poudyr of pepyr & a lytyl salt & rol hit up ther yn put hem on a broch rost hem yf thu wilte thu may endore hem & make hem a service or els put hem in wyn and halfe so much of fresch broth & do hem in a pot to gedyr with hole clovys macys herbes & onions hewyn small with poudrys safron & salt aley hit up with sause gynger or galantyn stew hit to gedyr and serve hit forthe for a sewe.

[62.] Pyke in sauce
Dyght a pyke and take the pouch and the fee seth hem in halfe wyn and halfe watyr cast ther to perceley onyons mynsyd smal lete the onyons & the herbes boyle to gedyr & seth the pyke sause & as hit sethyth blow of the grane & cast hit to the pouch & the fee and take payndemayn or othir tendyr bredde & cut hit in the maner of brues & tost hit on a rost yryn then minse the pouch & the fee but fyrst boyle sause gynger with the pouch and the fee to aley hit with al & cast ther to a good quantite of poudyr of gynger salt & safron and a good quantite of vergeus then cast thy brew in to a charger & the pyke a bovyn & cast the sauce of the pouch & the fee uppon the pyke in dysches & serve hit forth.

[63.] Turbut rostyd in sauce
Cut a way the fynes of the turbut & cut the fysch in maner of a hastelyng put hit on a rounde broche when hit ys halfe rostyd cast ther yn smal salt take vergeus or venygger & wyn & poudyr of gynger & a lytyll canell & cast ther on in the rostyng & have a vessell ther undyr to kepe the styllyons down & cast hit on aghen when hit is rostyd ynowghe hete the same sause & cast hit on the fisch yn dischys al hote.

[64.] Salmon rostyd in sauce
Cut a salmon yn rounde pecys roste hem on a roste yryn take wyne & poudyr of canell & draw hem thorow a streynour & minse onyons small & do togedyr boyle hit take venyger or vergeys and poudyr of pepyr gynger & salt & do ther to ley the samon on disches & poure the syrippe a bovyn & serve hit forth.

[65.] Brawn in confyte

Seth fresch brawn till hit be y nowghe than paryt grynd hit in a morter temper hit up with almond milke draw hit thorow a streyner into a pott do ther to sygire & poudyr y nowe of clovys let hit boyle take floure of canell [f.63v] and poudyr of clowys a god quantite do ther to boyle hit do ther to poudyr of gynger take hit oute of the pott & do hit in a lynnyn cloth & presse hit ther yn than lech hit fayre but nott to thynne then take ribbys of a bore al bare & shote hem endelong thorow the leches & serve forth a lech or ij yn a dysch.

[66.] Leche Lumbard

Boyle datys in swete wyne grynd hem draw hem with th same wyne as chargeaunt as ye may do hem yn a pott with sygure boyle hit put ther to poudour of gynger & canell a grete dele stere hit welle to gedyr yf be nowghte styfe ynowghe put ther to hard yolkes of eyron or gratyd bredde or els thu may boyle brawn & draw hit thorow a streynoure with out any lycour in the boylyng do hit to gedyr also thu may do with al maner of lech lumbard that thu makyste and yn lentyn tyme thu may have of sundez of stockfisch when hit ys boyled take out of the pott do hit on a bord presse hit to gedyr when hit ys colde cut hit in brede leches & serve hit forth a lech or ij in a dysch & poudyr a lytyll clarre aboven.

[67.] Tayle

Take a lytyll milke of almonds drawyn up with wyn & do hit in a pott do ther to figes reysens & datys cut and sygure & good pondys boyle hit up colour hit with safron & messe hit forth.

[68.] Blaunche de sorre

Blaunch almonds grynd hem draw hem with swete broth make a thike mylke take brawn of capons tendyr sodyn hewyn small & grounden & temper hit up with sume of the mylke & put ther to sygure y nowghe & boyle hit as mortrus take sume of thy milke boyle hit & cast hit on a cloth as crem & have out clene the watyr & putt hit in to that othir & a ley hit up ther with put ther to a cupfull of swete wyn loke that hit be salt & serve hit forthe and on fisch days take pyke or haddocke wel sodyn or codlyng & do awey the skyn & the bones & make hit in the same maner as thu dedyst the othir & draw thy mylke with the broth of fresch congure.

[69.] Blaw maungere

Take a thike mylke of almonds blaunched & drawyn up with fayre watyr grynd ryce draw hem with the milke take brawn of capons fesauntes or of pertrysch sodyne tendyr & tesyd smalle put ther to sygure & salt loke hit be stondyn & dresse hit forth as ryse cut almonds in lenye frye hem a lytyll & medyll hem with sygure & plant clovys a bovyn and on fysch dayes take pyke or haddoke welle sodyn & pyke the fysch for the bones & rubbe hit in a streyner with youre hond that hit be [f.64r] smalle and do hit in the stede of fysh.

[70.] Blaunch Doucet

Take brawn of capons groundyn & drawyn up with wyne & do hit in a pot with a lytyll hony or sygure and aley hit with almonds & poudyr of gynger & couch ther on yolkes of eyron and on fysch dayes take perche pyke or haddok or othir good fysch worch hit up in the same maner & make pelett of past & put ther on as thu dost yolkes of eyron.

[71.] Chikeney

Do almonde mylke yn a poot take cornels of okekornes rostyde grynd hem draw hem with wyn or ale do ther to a grete porcyon of sigure saundres & safron & othir poudrs & seson hit up with poudres & the schelles & set a bovyn.

[72.] Blanke desire

Take yolkes of eyron sodyn hard & safron & bred growndyn with cow milke boyl do ther to white of eyron cut smal & spyndez of porke corven ther to aley hit a lytyll with raw yolkes of eyron.

[73.] Dage

Take porke groundyn & ryse cryndd & do hit in a pott with broth of the same porke with saundres poudyr & sygure sesyn hit up with venyger when hit ys y dressyd cast on almondys fryed & cuttyd gyngour mynsyd & poudyr of gyngour.

[74.] Sypers

Take porke sodyn grynd hit temper hit up with milke of almondys drawyn withe broth & a perty of wyn or els a lytyll venyger do ther yn fygez & reysons of coraunce sigure & safron & salt boyle hit up

with yolkes of eyron when hit ys y boylyd do yn poudyr of gynger
& messe hit forthe as mortruys & cast drage a bovyn.

[75.] Floreye

Take flourys of rosys wesch hem & grynd hem with almond mylke
take brawn of capons groundyn & do ther to loke hit be stondyng
cast ther yn sygure & cast ther on the leves of floure of the rose &
serve hit forth.

[76.] Creme boyled

Take swete creme of melke do hit in a pott do ther to butter
clearyfyed set hit on the fyre stere hit when hit boyles have yolkes
of eyron drawyn thorowgh a streynour in to a boyle & put boylyng
coem ther to [f.64v] with a ladyl styr hit well for quallyng & put hit
in the pott a ghen & yf be nedd gheve hit a lytyl more of the fyre
loke hit have white sygure y nowghe & of the batture also loke hit
be standyng as mortrues & coloure hit with safron loke hit be salt
messe hit forth and strew on poudour of gynger.

[77.] Lyed mylke

Take cow mylke & sugure do hit on a pott set hit over the fyre
whan hit boyleth a ley up with yolkes of eyroun & loke hit be
rennyng & not to chargeaunt take whete brede & cut hit on chyves
do hem yn disches loke thy mylke be salt & poure hit a bovyn.

[78.] Moretruys of wresch fysch

Take hound fisch haddoc or codlyng sodyn pyke hit clene fro the
bonnys take a wey the skyn grynd the lyver ther with grynd
almonds with fresch fisch broth make a good mylke of almonds y
blanched temper up the fisch ther with take payndemayn gratyd or
sigure ther with set hit on the fyre when hit boyleth loke hit be
stond[ing] messe hit forth & strew on blaunch poudour.

[79.] Mortruys of flesch

Take brawn of capons & porke sodyn & groundyn tempyr hit up
with milke of almonds drawn with the broth set hit on the fyre put
to sigure & safron when hit boyleth take som of thy mylke boylyng
from the fyre & aley hit up with yolkes of eyron than hit be ryght
chargeaunt styre hit wel for quellyng put ther to that othyr & stere

hem to gedyr & serve hem forth as mortruys and strew on poudyr of gynger.

[80.] Blaunch mortruys of fisch
Take haddok codlyng or thornebak sodyn pyke out the bonys do a way the skyn grynd the fisch make a mylke of almonds y blaunchyd & temper up the fisch ther with take payndemayn gratyd & sigure ther withe set hit on the fyre whan hit boyleth loke hit be ston messe hit forth & strew on blaunch poudyr.

[81.] Blaunch mortruys
Take brawn of capons pertriches or fesaunts sodyn tendyr hewe hit small on a bordd grynd hit take a mylke of almonds yblaunchid & do as dost with the fysch.

[82.] Paynd foundow
Take bred frye hit in grece or yn oyle put yn rede wyne & grynd hit with reysons & draw hit with claryfyed hony & gryre [gleyre] of eyron & watyr scom hit clene & put hit to that othir do ther to clovys macez & gynger mynsed [f.65r] & good poudyr & salt loke hit be stondyng & floresch hit with anies in confite.

[83.] Caudell
Draw yolkes of eyron thorow a streynour with wyne or with ale that hit be ryght rennyng put ther to sigure safron & no salt bet well to gedyr set hit on the fyre on clene colys stere welle the bottom & the sydys tyl hit be ynowghe scaldyng hote thu shalle fele be they when hit begynnys to com then take hit of and styre alwey fast & yf be nedd alay hit up with som of the wyne or yf hit com to hastyly put hit in cold watyr to mydsyd of the pot & stere hit alwey fast & serve hit forth.

[84.] Caudell fery
Draw yolkes of eyron thorow a streynour take a thyn mylke of almonds draw yn with bastard or with osey or with swete wyn set hit on the fyre stere hit well when hit ys at the boylyng have yolkes of eyron in a bolle drawyn thorow a streynour let wyn ther to & stere evermore welle for quellyng tyl hit be aleyed so that hit be stondyng if outzlef[?] of the wyn kepe hit put thy caudell in to the pott & yf hit be nede set hit on the fyre steryng alwey make hit

nowghte to hote for quellyng yf hit be chargeaunt aley hit with the remenant of the wyn dresse hit as a stondyng potage and strew on blaunch poudyr thu mayst yf thu wilt draw payndemayn & make hit up in the maner or thu mayst yf thu wilt set clene wyne at the fyre & when hit ys at boylyng have yolkes of eyron drawyn thorow a streynour in to a bolle put wyne ther to sygure & safron loke hit be stondyng serve hit & strew on blaunch poudyr.

[85.] Charlet
Do cow mylke in a pott have porke sodyn tendyr or of a loyn of vele hew hit smal do ther to safron & salt set hit over the fyre when hit ys at the boylyng have yolkes of eyron drawyn thorow a streynour put ther wyne or ale bet hit to gedyr put hit to the mylke stere hit when hit begynnys to a ryse set hit fro the fyre let hit crud well serve hit forthe iij or iiij leches in a dysch with the wheye yf thu wylt have hit in for sayd ley hit over a cloth over a bord & presse hit to gedyr lik thes y hav out cut hit in levys or smal pecys & ley iij or iiij in a dysch grynd almonds unblaunched & draw up a thike milke with wyne put to poudyr of gynger safron canel & sigure a grete dele sawndres & salt hole clovys & macys & set hit over the fyre stere hit when hit ys at boylyng take hit of & poure over the charlette. [f.65v]

[86.] Perys in confyte
Take hony boyle hit a lytill do ther yn sigure poudyr of galentyn & clovis brucet[?] anneyce safron & saundris & cast ther yn the peris sodyn & paryd & cutt in pecys & wyn & venyger sesyn hit up with poudyr of canell so that be broun ynow [m?]ake whentheses in the same maner al but venyger & put ther to clovys & macys and ys thu will take datys mynsed & do ther to & colour hit with safron.

[87.] Perys in composte
Take wyn & a grete dele of canell with sygure set hit on the fyre lat hit not boylyng draw hit thorow a streynour leche datys thyn & do ther to in a panne or in a pott aley hem with chard quyns & salt loke hit be doucet & chargeaunt do hit out of that vessell in to a trene vessell & let it kele pare smal reysons take trydd gyngour paryd & temper hym ij days or iij in wyne & aftyr ward ley hym in claryfyd hony cold a day and nexte than take the reysons out of the

hony & cast ther to perys in composte & serve hit forth with the syrip al cold.

[88.] Perys in Syrup
Boyle wardons that they be somdell tendyr pare hem cut hem yn pecys take canell a grete dele draw hit thorow a streynour iij or iiij tymys with good wyn in a pott do ther to sygure a grete dele poudyr of gynger anneys clovis & macys and yf thu wilte datys mynsyd & reysons of coraunce set hit on the fyre when hit boyleth cast yn the perys lete hem boyle to gedyr when hit ys boyled y nowghe loke hit be broun of canell & put ther to poudyr of gynger a grete dele loke hit be somdele doucet & serve hit forth.

[89.] Brawn ryal brawn sypres brawn bruse
Take fresh brawn boyle hit in fayre watyr till hit be tendour blanche almondys grynd hem draw hem up with the same broth & a perty of wyn as hote as thu may than make thu milke hote & do thy brawn in a streynour hot & draw hit with the mylke hott do ther to sygure a grete dele venyger set hit on the fyre boyle hit salt hit do hit in a vessel when hit ys cold yf thu nowte have hit out of the vessel with out hote watyr or a ghenst the fyre ley a cloth on a bord & turne the vessell upsodowne ther on & schake the vessell that hit falle oute cut ther in the lech & serve hit forthe iij or iiij in a dysch & strew on poudyr of gynger or paryd gynger [f.66r] mynsyd with anneyce clovys macys & annys in confite yf thu wilt thu may draw som ther of with the same broth & with a perty of wyne with out mylke colourd as bryght as lambur with any colour safr saffron hem when hit ys cold & floresch that othir ther with or els thu mayst cut that othir hit in leches as thu doste that othir & serve hit forth in same maner or thy may turne hit in othir colour yf thu wilt have a grene draw hit with mylke of almonds in to a morter & safron ther with or els put safron when hit ys growndyn muche or lytyll aftur thu wylt make thi colour & colour hit ther with when thu takysthit from the fyre & do ther with as thu dedyst with the todyr and yf thy wile thu may do ther yn poudres or thu may put ther yn a grete quantyte of canell & of gynger & of sawndres to make hit brown & serve hit forthe in the same maner or yf thu wilt thu may take tursele & wesch hit & grynd hit well in wyn that thu sesonyste hit up withe and when hit ys boylyd coloure hit up with bloure sangueyn whethir thu wilt & do ther with as thu dedist with

the tothyr or thu may yf thu wilt when thu takyst hit fro the fyre &
have al seson hit have brawn sodyn tendyr & when hit ys cold cut
hit in leches or dyse hit & cast hit in the pott & stere hit to gedyr &
put hit in to that othyr pott vessell when hit ys cold lech hit & do
ther with as thu dodyst with that othir & serve hit forth.

[90.] Brawn ryall

Take the soundes of stokfisch dry & lay hem in watyr iij days &
every day change the watyr than take hem up & lay hem on a bord
& scharpe hem clene withe the egge of a knyf wesch hem & sethe
hem in fayre watyr then take hem up & sethe hem in broth of
fresch fysch as of conger til they be tendyr or als in the same watyr
and put ther to elys to amend the broth then take blaunch
almondys grynd hem with the same broth hote & make up the
soundes & grynd hem wyth the same broth & yf thu wilt thu may
take som of the elys ther to & temper hem up with the broth hote
draw hit as hote as thu may suffyr thy hond ther yn thu mau make
hit in al maner as thu makyste brawn of flesch. And yf thu wilt
seson hit with the white of eyron breke hem at the grete ende & do
out al that ys in the eye wesch the shell drye hem & sett hem on the
salt upryght & put ther yn som of the white braune take som of the
same braun colourd with safron & medlyd with poudres put ther
yn pepenys of the gretnys of a neye yolke & fil hit with [f.66v] the
braun that hit stond full when hit ys cold peyl of the shyll set hit in
salt as eggez or in crispis and pych hem with clovys a bovyn iiij or v
& fill up with blaunch poudyr & serve hem forthe in the stede of
egges in he same maner thu may do with brawn in flesch tyme or
thu may yf hit somdell of poudyr of gynger & chaunge the colour
as thu dedyst braun in flesch tyme.

[91.] Betrayn yn lentyn

Take the braun that thu makyst yn lentyn do ther to poudyr of
pepyr poudyr of clovys & poudyr of canell a grete dele loke hit be
broun of saunderes yf thu wilt take blaunched almonds & dyse hem
in a perty of wyne & a perty of venyger & do to gedyr when hit
boyleth put hit out in to a nothir vessell when hit ys cold lech hit
serve hit forth as thu doyst braun ryall.

[92.] Betreyn in flesch tyme

Take calves feet clene scalyd set hem in wyne & a perty of swete
broth that thay be tendyr take hem up on a bord pyke a way the

29

bonys kep som for senewys hew hem al to gedyr grynd hit temper
hit up with the self broth do hit in a pot dyse the senewys blaunch
almond and poudyr of pepyr poudyr of clovys & a lytyll poudyr of
canel a grede dele of saundrys & yf thu wilt of safron a lytyll set hit
on the fyre & when hit boyleth put ther to yolkes of eyron dysyd
smal & poudyr of gynger venyger & salt put hit on a vessell when
hit ys cold leche hit & serve hit forth.

[93.] Storgeon for sopers
Take calvys fete & flesch of the hed & the longes sodyn tendyr hew
hem smal tempyr hem up with the same broth or yf thu wylt thu
may gnde [grind?] hit & tempyr hit well and strew on foulys of
percelleye & do ther to poudyr of pepyr poudyr of clovys yf thu
wylt & salt & boyle hit to gedyr & ley hit on a clene bord & kepe
hit well to gedyr that hit ren nought a brod when hit ys cold cut hit
in leches do venyger yn boyle onyons mynsyd & foules of
percelleye & poudyr of gynger ley the leches ther yn & when thu
sendyst hem ley ij or iij in a dysch & somdell of the sauce ther with.

[94.] Cold lech viaund
Take quynses boyled pare hem pike out the buyst cut hem yn pecys
do hem in a pott of erth do ther to white grece that hony or sygure
ys put yn & aley hem up with hony claryfydd & raw yolkes of eyren
& a lytyll almond mylke do ther to poudres of safron & lech hit
fayre.

[95.] Lech lumbard
Claryfye hony put ther to poudyr lat hit boyle longe put ther to
almonds [f.67r] cut smal and gradyd bred that hit be chargeaunt
stere hit well to gedyr lat hit nought boyle to longe for brennyng of
the almondys take gratyd bred & strew on a clene borde take hit
out of the pott & lay ther on & strew on more gratyd bred and
couch hit to gynger gedyr that hit ren nought a brod when hit ys
cold cut hit in brod leches & serve forth ij or iij yn a dysch & strew
on poudyr of gynger If thu may hete hit have smal konenys by fore
& poure hit ther yn & serve hit in the stede of cold bakemete or yf
thu wilt poure hit by hit sylf and crem of almonds or els mylke a
stondyng potage of quynsys or of fruet colourd yolow & fil hit up
that othir syde & strew ther on anneys in confyte & othir dragge
what thu wylte & serve hit forth cold.

[96.] Cold bruet of rabets

Grynd reysons or datys draw hem up with osey put ther to creme of almond & poudyr of canel a grete dele drawyn with swete wyn poudyr lumbard poudour of greynez & poudyr of gynger & a lytyll of venyger a swete sygure set hit on the fyre when hit ys boylyng take hit of & put hit in a boll have rabets boyled & that in good broth & salt take hem unlace hem by the bake fro thy bonys on both sydes ley hem in a sewe serve hem forth ley hem in dyshys & poure on the sewe ther to serve hit forth & yf thu wylt thu may chop hem in pecys & yf thu have chikenys reys the whynges & the thyes of hem kepe hem & chop the body & when hit ys in the sewe serve hit forthe in the same maner as sewe qyall.

[97.] Dyvers desire

Grynd reysons draw hem up with osey othir with swete wyn that hit ve somdele thyn do hit in a pott mynse datys & do ther to & reysons of coraunse clovys macys poudyr of pepyr & poudyr lombard & sigure take pyggez clene y schallyd or kede or lomb or konyng or chikenes choppyd small in pecys & frye hit & do hit to gedyr boyle hit & sesyn hit up with poudyr of gynger & salt & yf thu wilt take venyger & make hit egyr & serve hit forth & yf thu wylt grynd almondes & do in the same maner & coloure hit with turnesole othir let hit be white whethir thu wilt and yf thu may make past of eyron & paryd floure make yn thy foyle & boyle hit in small pelets or els in pelys & fry hem in white grece lat the flesch be out & when the sew boyleth do hit ther to & serve hit forth or yf thu wylt make foyles of past & couche ther yn foyl flesch of capons & porke sodyn & groundyn & seson hit up with poudres & salt make pelets ther of eche [f.67v] pelet as grete as a fynger loke hit be well y closyd & frydd put hit in dysches & poure the syrip abovyn & let no venyger come ther yn yf thu wilt have a stondyng potage ther of draw hit more chargeaunt & draw hit forth as mortrewys that thu makyst of reysons & of the same colour as that othir ys before & do parte the othir in the dysches and yf thu wylt make ther of a bakyn thu may put everych of them by hem sylf or els depart that on with that othir & serve hit forth whethir thy wylt hote or cold & strew ther on a dragge of paryd gynger mynsyd & anys in confite & blaunch poudyr & serve hit forth whetyr hit be in the forme of potage or of bakyn mete in what kind that thu wylt thu may hit & a ley hit with yolkes of eyron yf thu lyst aftyr the

boylyng take som of the same & set hit on the fyre yn a pott & at
the boylyng have yolkes of eyron drawn thorow a streynour in to a
bolle & poure yn the wyn softely & rennyng & stere hit s fast in the
bolle for quellyng & loke that hit be ryght chargeaunt of yolkes &
put hit in to that other sewe that ys made by fore ster hit well to
gedyr do hit forth loke no venyger come ther on loke hit be doucet
& som dele bytyng of the poudres and yf thu wilt make hit of fisch
thu mayse in the same maner as thu dedist the flesch take calvour
samon base & melet splattyd & choppyd in pecys & frydd & do
ther with as thu dost with the flesch or take a perch or els haddok
or base sodyn pike out the bonys grynd hit & medyll hit with good
poudres & salt & make hit in rounde pelets than have a batire of
mylke of almondys put the pelets ther yn take hem up & frye hem
yn hole rolle hem rounde ley hem in disches & poure the syrip a
bovyn and yf thu lyst thu maist do with flesch yn the same maner.

[98.] Viaund ryall

Grynd reysons draw with bastard clare osey or othir swete wyn the
best thu may gete take datys cut grete reysons of coraunce clovis
macys pynes & floure of canel yf thu have hit pure hit in a pot &
som of the good wyn ther with when hit ys boyled y nowghe take
the syrip of the resons & the creme of almonds & past ryall &
pynad and gobet ryal & gynger in confite & claryfyd quynsys or
chard wardys poudyr poudyr of canell do al thes to gedyr yn a pot
set hit on the fyre stere hit wel when hit ys at the boylyng take hit
of loke hit be doucet and that hit have y nowgh of poudres &
somdell of salt deresse hit forth as a flate potage & yf thu serve hit
forth colour hit with blossemys of safron have fisch braune sodyn
tendyr & draw yn thorowgh a streynour & colour hit with safron
that hit be as brythe as lambur when hit ys cold floresch the sewe
ther with in dysches & serve hit forthe.

[99.] Mawmene ryall

Grynd reysons & draw up in the same maner of wynes as thu
dydist that othir by [f.68r] fore put ther to crem of almonds do hit
in a pot take al kyndes of hote spyces as thu didist to that othir &
parid gynger & datys cut & sygure claryfyed & put hit in a pot to
gedyr with some of the wyne & boyle hit with some of the same
wyne to gedyr & take hit of & put hit to gedyr to that othir & put
ther to poudyr of canell poudyr of gynger of lumbard & othir good

poudres set hit on the fyre stere hit well when hit ys at the boylyng
take hit of loke hit be doucet & yf hot have any of poudyr loke thu
have brawn of capons fesauntes or pertryggs sodyn tendyr & tesyd
small put ther to lat hit be nought stondyng loke hit be brown of
canell saundres & safron & messe hit forth as a flate potage &
florysch hit with sygure plate strewyd uppon when hit ys boyled
loke no leve of the fyre ryse aboven the viaunt ryall for brennyng
of the sewe.

[100.] Gely on fysch days
Splat pekys & tenches chop hem in small pecys & draw smal
perchys fle elys chop hem & do to gedyr in a pan & boyle hoit with
rede wyne take hit up ley hit on a clene cloth or on a clene bord
pyle out the bonys strip the sknyn kepe the pecys hole couch hem
in dischys the pyke & the tenche to gedyr & the gobenys of the elys
& stryp the skyn a wey of the perchis & couch hem put one in a
dysch & othir charge nowght thi dyschis over muche with youre
fisch set hit on a colde place ther they may stond styll & set the
panne aghene over the fyre & take barbell or congure playce or
thornebake or othir good fisch that wil a gely & loke the skynys of
the elys be clene & do ther to boyle hit in the same broth skeme hit
clene that ther be no fat of the fisch ther on take hit up with a
skemer do hit where thu wilt poure the broth thorow a clene cloth
in to a clene pott set hit aghen on the fyre do ther to poudyr of
pepyr & longe pepyr brekyd in a morter & thu may yf thu wilt have
smal bagges of lynnyn cloth iij or iiij & put youre poudres ther yn
sew hem that they go nought out henge over the sydys of the
panne when ye boyle youre fisch a way tyl the seson hit take hem
out & wryng out the broth & do hem awey & that ys bettyr maner
then take up some ther of & poure hit on the brerd of a disch & let
hit be cold & ther thu shalt se where hit be chargeaunt or els take
more fisch that wolle gely & put hit ther yn do a wey the fisch
sesyn the broth with venyger & salt colour with watyr of safron
that hath be longe sokyd to gedyr so that the watyr have drawn out
al the colour of the safron & shall kepe youre gely clere & bryght as
lambour do on a drop or ij on the brede of a dysch & ther thu shalt
a se yf that thy coloure be good salt hit take a clene clothe bynde
the corners hong hit up poure the gely ther yn have a vessell undyr
nethe kepe that rennought fyl up your dysches ther with when the
most hete hit [f.68v] splat hit with blaunched almonds that they

33

may hong ther yn and hole clovys & macys when hit ys cold florych hit with paryd gynger & serve hit forthe.

[101.] Cristell gely

Take swete wyn that wol hold his colour & boyle youre fisch ther yn & do ther with yn alle maners as thu dost with that othir & gheve hit none othir colour than shalt thu have hit as brygth as silvyr & serve hit forth.

[102.] Gely of flesch

Take conyngys fle hem scalle pyggys chopp hem fre of the here scale chikenys draw hem & yf thu wilt thu may chopp kede also the conynge & the pygge couch hit in dyschys in a cold place ther they may stond styll set thy broth a gen ovir the fyre loke hit be wel skemyd that no fat be ther on take calvys feete clene scaldyd clene hem set hem in the same broth tyl they be tendyr loke thy brothe be clene skemyd sesyn hit in al maner as thy dose thy fysch & fill thy disches ther with & do ther to in al maner as thy dost to fysch.

[103.] Creme of almondys

Blaunch grynd hem kepe hem as white as thy may & tempyr hem up with thike mylke with fayre watyr drawe hit put hit in a clene pott sette hit on the fyre stere hit well when hit by gynneth to seth take hit of yf thy have moch do ther to a dischfull of wyn venyger yf ther be a lytyll do ther yn to the pott lete hyt stond a whyle have a clene cloth holden on a bord by twyxt ij men or iiij men strat cast the creme ther yn with a ladyll as brod as they cloth & rubbe thy cloth undyr neth with a ladyll toward [crossed out: the] & froward so that thy may draw out all the watyr then gedyr hit to gedyr in to the myddyl of the cloth & bynd the corners to gedyr honge hit on a pynne & lett the watyr soke out do hit on a bolle & tempyr hit up with white wyn bose hit with a sawcer til hit be as softe as thy wolt have hit.

[104.] Hages of Almayne

Take eyron draw hem thorow a streynour perboyle percelley in fat broth hew & hard yolkes of eyron to gedyr do ther to poudyr of gynger sigure & salt & marye & put hit in a streynour ende in a boylyng pott perboyle hit take hit up lat hit kele cut hit smal take drawn eyron put hem in a panne loke they pan be moysty of grece

34

lat the bature ren a brod into a foyle cuch ther yn hard yolkes
merye & percellye & turne the iiij sydds to gedyr that hit close a
bovyn & ley hit square take of the same bature & wete the eggys
that hit hold stonch & close ther yn the stuf turne hit upsodown
frye hit on both sydys & serve hit forthe.

[105.] Quystes
Take a pese of befe or of motyn wyn & watyr boyle hit skeme hit
clene than take quystes chop hem with yn with hole pepyr & cast
hem in to the pott & let hem stew ryght well to gedyr & take
poudyr of gynger & a lytyll vergeys & salt [f.69r] & cast ther to do
hem in fayre dischys a quyst or ij in a disch for a maner of potage
and when thu shalt serve hit forth take a lytyll broth & put hit in
dischys to the quystys.

[106.] Vontes
Take gobets of mary & dates cut sigure & poudyr of gynger a grete
dele & safron & salt & make a foyle as thu makest to that othir by
fore & do hit out of the panne & than make a nothir take of the
forsayd stuf & couch in al most as brod as the foyle & wete the
bredys of the foyle a bovyn close hit late it bake forth esyly when
hit ys bakyn cut hit in pecys ech off ij & serve hit forth.

[107.] Bastons
Make a stif bature of yolkes of eyron & paryd floure & sigure a
grete dele & a lytyll yest of new ale set hit by the fyre or els in a pot
boylyng that hit may take a lytyl hete when hit ys rysyd sweng hit
well to gedyr that hit a ghene loke thy oven be hote & clene
swepyd poure hit on the floure of the oven & bake hit as french
bred than make hit out cut a wey the crustys abovyn the bred of a
nobyll & make an hole & reys hit al abovyn under the crust endlyng
ovyrtugharte [over thwart] as thike as thu may with a knyf & so do
enyure to the boyfound [bottom] but safe the boyfound [bottom]
hole & the crust al a boute & fil hit full of claryfyde hony & set on
the crust a ghen & set hym on the oven when they be somdell
drydd & serve hit forth.

[108.] Samatays
Take vellyd cruddys or they be pressyd do hem yn a cloth wryng
out the whey do hem yn a morter grynd hem well with paryd floure

35

& tempyr hem with eyryn & creme of cow mylke & make ther of a
rennyng bature than have white grece in a panne loke hit be hote
take up the bature with a saucer & let hit renne in the grece draw
thyn hond bacward [crossed out: than] that hit may renne [crossed
out: bacward] a brode then fry hem ryght well & somdell hard
reschelyng & serve hit forth in disches & strew on white sygure.

[109.] Long Fryturys
Make of the same but lat no creme come ther yn loke hit be more
styf aftyr ley hit on a clene bord that ys no broddyr than theyn
hond take a bone of the ryb of a best wete hym in grece that thy
bature cleve nought ther on & stryke of the bature yn to a pan that
hit may fal in to smal gobets every fretyre of hondfull longe &
serve hem forth hote & strew on white sygure thu may grynd
tendyr chese & make freturys in the same maner and yf thu wilt
take sodyn porke sodyn tendour & grynd hit ther with make hit in
pelets as grete as a negge & that ys freture lumbard.

[110.] Payn purdyeu
Take paundemayn or fresh bredd pare a wey the crustys cut hit in
schyverys fry hem [f.69v] a lytyll yn claryfyd hony buture have
yolkes of eyron drawyn thorow a streynour & as hote as thu may
ley the brede ther yn that hit be al helyd with bature then fry in the
same bature & serve hit forth & strew on hote sygure.

[111.] Ffelets of porke yn doryd
Do awey the skyn of felets of porke & broch hem roste hem take
poudyr bast hem take yolkes of eyron drawyn thorow a streynour
when the felets be rostyd dry hem that no grece be rennyng uppon
hem & endore hem with yolkes of eyron a fore sayde.

[112.] Hattes
Make a past of paryd floure knedyn with yolkes of eyron & make a
st[uff] of vele or pork sodyn & gryoundyn with yolkes of eyron
mary dysyd & datus mymynsyd corauns sigure safron & salt poudyr
& medyll al to gedyr & make youre past of round foyles of the
brode of a saucer as thyn may be drawn turne hem doble that the
brerdys may come to the medyll of the foyle then turne hem to
gedyr that the brerdys on the more mete al aboute & the lasse
brerde turne upward with outyn in the maner of a hat & close well

the egges that they hold well fyll ther on thy stuff have a bature of yolkes of eyron & whete floure in the opyn syde that ys toward loke ther yn the stuf be closyd & set hit yn hote grece upryght when the bature ys fryed thu may ley hym down & fry hym al over.

[113.] (Hattes) In lentyn
Thou may make thy past of paryd floure knodyn with milke of almondys & put ther to alytyll safron take fresch samon base melete & the lyver of fisch sodyn & groundyn & a lytyll fruyte ther with & yf thu wilte poudrys safron & salt make thy bature of paryd floure & milke of almondys & dryght hit in the same maner as thu dedyste byfore.

[114.] Sauce Madam
Take the yarmazs of a gose flat hem wesch hem skinyn hem clene and the gessez and the lyne & the lefe of the gose & the soule do al in a pot to gedyr boyle hit tendyr take hit up lay hit on a bord pyke a wey the bonys of the whengys & hew hit smal do hit in a pott do ther to onyons mynsyd smal clovys macys & fars the gose with onyons & herbys hewyn wardons mynsyd grapys rose hepe smyte here in pecys lay here in a chargeour & do the farsour in a pott to that othir & wyn & sesyn hit up with poudr salt & venyger and yf thu wilt thu may take yolkes of eyron sodyn hard & ground small & do ther to like hit be salt & pure hit on the perys.

[115.] Sauce camelyn for quaylys & othir maner of foules and fysch
[f.70r] Take white bred & draw hit in the maner of sauce gynger with venyger & put ther to poudyr of canell a grete dele & poudyr of gynger & poudyr lumbard & draw hit a ghen & yf thu wilt draw a lytyll mustard ther with & sesyn hit up with sygure that hit be doucete salt hit & colour hit with safron.

[116.] Chaudon of Swan or of wylde goose
Take the hert of a swan the geser and the yarmez slete hem shave hem seth hem & the fetys & the whyngys also take out the bonnys of the whyngys do hem awey hew al that othir small do hit in a pot sethe hit with the same broth draw a lyour of brede with rede wyn alay hit up ther with & sesyn hit up with poudyr of peper gyngour & salt loke hit have a good colour of blod take out the smal bonys

of thy fete & lete the flesch be over the leggys a bovyn & ley a fete in a dysch & put chaudon a boven.

[117.] Wellyd pepyr for rostyd veele
Cut brede in shivys tost hem on a roste yryn that hit be somdele broun yf thu wylte thu may grate hit or els temper hit wyn or with ale & draw hit thorow a streynour that hit be somdele thike put ther to poudyr of pepyr & a lytyl safron boyle hit & serve hit forth hot loke hit have a taste of venyggour.

[118.] Fresch lamprey bakyn
Take lamprey do hem in a pott do ther to a porcyon of rede wyne & stop the pott a bovyn that the lepe nought out when he ys endyng take hym out & put hym in scaldyng watyr & take hym in a lynnen cloth in thy hond & a handfull of hey in that othir hond & strip hem well that alle the glame go a wey & save the skyn hole then wesch hym & kepe hym clene & cut hym a lytyll over twarte a straw brede by fore the navyll so that the stryng be lose then slete hym a lytyll at the throte & take out the stryng & save the blode in a vessell yf he be a female thrist hym in thy honde from the navill upward so that the spaune come out there that take out the stryngys yf thu wilte bone hym slyte hym a lytyll in the same place with yn so that thu may come to the bone & louse the bone with a pyke fro thy fysch & as esyly as thu may drawe awey the bone fro thy tayle that hit come out hole & wynd the bone aboughte youre hond & alwey as hit comith out w wynd hit up & gedyr hit out hole aftyrward othe ch thy lamprey outward over the bake syde eche pece iij fyngerys brode ofn lynye so that hit hold to gedyr & toyle hym well in his oune blode yf thu wilte make thyn be somdele brown & take good wyn to the bakyng of the lamprey & halfe pynte will one to youre brede theryn draw hit make hit nought to chargeaunt yf thu wilte thu may draw a few reysons & draw hit up with than loke the fiste paerte be venygger do ther to poudyr of canell a grete dele poudyr of galentyn poudyr lumbard poudyr gynger sawndres sigure saffron & salt yf thu wilt lev [f.70v] hit be thyn brown & yolowe make thy colour more of saundres make a large kosyne of paryd floure do youre lamprey ther yn & poure in galentyne so that hit stond as hye as the lamprey loke hit have a good lyde & a wete the brerdys al a boute & ley uppon put a penne by twyne the lede & the cofine & close hit al aboute till you come

to the penne then blow thy penne that the syde ryse al aboute then take out thy penne close hit fast then have a good pele & sethit esyly on the oven & bake hit esyly & longe sokyng To make soppys in galentyn in a vessell & put ther to wyn & medle hit to gedyr till hit be smoth do sigure and yf hit nede put to more poudyr & medyll in fere that hit be somdele thyn then put hit in a pott of erthe set hit on colys of fyre tyll hit be at boylyng & stere hit well have white brede cut yn shyvers as brewys & tost hit a lytyll & then bast hit & poure some of the same galentyn in the same cofyne so that hit may wete the botom & couch ther some of youre brede & poure yn more galentyne then couche yn the remnaunt of youre brede & couch yn the remnaunt of youre galentyne & ley on the lede & serve hit forth.

[119.] Tartes of Flesch
Take porke sodyn pyke hit clene from thy bonys grynd hit small boyle fyggys in the broth of the flesch or yn wyn or in ale hew hit & grynd hit with eyron pare tendyr chese grynd hit to gedyr that the most perte stond by the flesch & the lest by the chese take pynes & reysons fry hem in a quantite of fresch grece & do hit in that othir with hole clowys macys & poudyr of pepyr & canell a grete dele & poudyr of gynger & sygure claryfyd or hony claryfyd safron & salt toyl hit well togedyr tyl thy grece be hote then make brode cofnys with the brerdys as thyn as thu may make hem thu nay chese of clovys or mynsyd datys whethir thu wilte medyl hem with the stuff or els strew hem above & ley on the ledys close hem & thu may put ther yn lyghte worke & make endoryng with mylke of almondys & safron & endore hem or thu bake hem.

[120.] Tartelets
Take small cofynys in the same maner as thu madyst that othir make thy stuf of boylyd fyges & spycys what thu wilte or yf thu wilte fisch or flesch & sesyn hit up in the same maner & fyll youre cofyns ther with ye may fry hem bake hem whethir ye wilt.

[121.] Bakyn purpays
Poudyr purpays perboyle hit well strip the skyn of take poudyr of pepyr canel yf hit be nede medyll hit with the fysch close hit up with foulys of past & bake hit venyson in the same maner.

[122.] Pyes of flesch capons and fesaunttes
Take good beef & sethe ther with pork wele or venyson hewyn
small do ther to [f.71r] poudyr of pepyr canell poudyr of clovis
gyngour & mynsyd datys yf thu wilee & reysons of coraunce &
medyll hit with venyggour safron & salt & take hit in thy moneys if
hit be welle sesond than couch hit in large cofyns & close yn
capons or fesauntes hole or yf thu wilte cut hit in pecys colour hem
well with safron & put ther yn othir wylde foule what thu wilte &
plant hit with half yolkes of eyron & strew on clovis macys & datys
mynsyd corans & quibibis close hem & bake hem longe & sokingly
& serve hem forth with the fyrst cource.

[123.] Crustad lumbard
Make large cofynys take datys pyke out the skynnys & yf thu wilte
thu may cut thy datys or els stop hem with blanch poudyr with yn
& do ther to grete gobets of marye & couch ther yn rabets with the
marye & small bryddys perboylyd well in fat broth & couch in ther
to clovis macys reysons of corauns & fry pynes & strew theron &
set hem yn ther own syrip of creme of cowmylke yolkes of eyron &
good poudyr sygure saundres safron & salt fyl hem ther with and
on fisch days boyle wardons tendyr or othir perys pare hem & hole
hem at the crown fil hem full of blaunch poudyr & turne yn the
pouydyr of gyngour that the poudyr lese ther yn & set hem in
cofyns & the stalkes upward & yf thu wilte thu may turne hem that
they be hid yn bature & fry hem or thu couch hem let no flesch
come ther to make thy syripe of thicke mylke of almondys make up
thu crustardys as thu dedyst on fisch days when they be bake yf thu
wilte thy may gylte the stalkys of the perys & syve hem forth.

[124.] Chauet of Beef
Take befe cut small do ther to poudyr of gyngour clovis & othir
good poudrys grapys vergys safron & salt toylyd to gedyr do
chikenys choppyd in coffyns & yolkes brockyd & cromyd small
bake hem & serve hem forth.

[125.] Chauet Ryall
Take marye cut yn grete gobets & couch hit in smal cofynnys &
small bryddys perboyle also ther with also and yf thu wilte rabets &
datys cut grete sigure vergeys safron & salt loke hit stond well by

the marye put to pousyr gyngour poudour lumbard close hem bake hem & serve hem forth.

[126.] Bakyn chikenes

Take chikenes clene skallyd trusse a sort as thu corouryst hem with wergeys safron & good poudyres couch hem in cofyns take salt lard of porke dysyd smal & medelyd with vergeys safron & salt & couch hem in the cofyns close hem & bake hem & serve hem forth.

[127.] Chauet yn fysch dayes

Take base melet or samon raw & take the fisch clene fro the bonys chop hit in pecys & couch hit in coffyns and eles with all take ther to all materes as thu dede to the noyte abovyn save on make thy syryp of thikke mylke of almondys as thu made that othir save yolkes [f.71v] of eyron set the coffyns in the oven fyl hem up with the serip & yf thu wile fry the fisch.

[128.] Darrolete

Take fysch mynsyd & almond mylke made with wyne & mynsyd brede saundres hony reysons poudres & safron medyl al to gedyr so that hit be thikke do hit in cofyns & bake hit in maner of flathyns.

[129.] Prineroll at pasche

Take blanch almondys & the floures of primeroll grynd hem temper hem up with swete wyne & with a perty of swete broth draw hit unto a thike mylke do hit in a pott sygure & salt & a lytyll safron that hit have the same colour as the primroll hath boyle hit & but hit be stondyng a ley hit with floure of ryse & serve forthe as stondyng potage & strew on primroll abovyn thu may yf thu wilt daperte hit in the disches dryssyng with rape ryall or with some othir stondyng sewe in.

[130.] To Make a Possote

Do cow mylke in a pott ovir the fyre when hit ys at boylyng putt in wyne or ale & no salt take hit from the fyre hele hit as sone as the crud ys gaderyd take uppe crud with a saucer or with a ladyell serve hit forth & strew on poudyr of gynger yf thu wilte thu may take the same crud & ley hit on a bord & presse out the whey & draw hit twyys or iij thorow a streynour with swete wyne put to poudyr of gynger & segure & medyll hit well to gedyr & serve hit forth as for a stondyng potage for soperys.

[131.] Pyes of Pares
Smyte fayre buttes of porke & of vele to gedyr & put hit in a pot with fresch broth & a quantite of wyne boyle all to gedyr tyl hit be ynow then put hit in a clene vessell put ther to raw yolkes of eyron poudyr of gynger sigure & salt mynsyd & reysons of corauns & make a fayre thin past & cofyns & do ther yn thy stuf & let hit bake y nowe & then serve hit forth.

[132.] Brinddy
Put wyne in to a pott & claryfydd hony saundres poudyr of pepyr canell clovis macys pynes datys mynsyd & reysons of corauns & cast ther to a lytyll venyggour set hit on the fyre lete hit boyle seth fygys in wyn grynd hem & draw hem thorow a streynour & cast ther to & let hem boyle to gedyr then take floure saferon sigure & salt make ther of kakes let hem be thyn ynowghe then cut hem lyke lysyngys & fry hem in oyle then put hem in to the syrip & loke the syrip be rennyng & serve hit forth.

[133.] Losyngys opyn
Make a past with paryd floure knedyn with watyr sigure safron & salt make hem in foyles then cut thy losyngs of the breed of thy hond or less frye hem in good oyle & serve hem forth foure or fyve yn a dysche. [f.72r]

[134.] Harbelet opyn
Smyte buttes of pork in pecys boyle hem in fayre watyr that they be ynowghe then do hem on a borde & do awey the skyn & the bonys hew hit small do hit in a fayre boll take ysope sage & percelly a grete quantite pike hit hew hit do hit in a vessell take fat of the same broth & do ther to boyle hit a lytyll & do to the flesch mynsyd datys clovis macys reysons of corauns pynes poudyr of gynger safron & salt & draw yolkes of eyron thorow a streynour put to sugure cull hem well to gedyr make rownd cofyns hardyn hem a lytyll in the oven then take hem out fill hem with a dysch full of the stuf set hem in the oven all opynly let hem bake thorow & serve hem forth.

[135.] Leche fryed
Take tendyr chese cut hit in shivers do hit in hote skallyng watyr when hit rennyth & yelleth to gedyr do a wey the watyr as clene as thu may & do ther ro claryfydd buttur al hote a grete dele & claryfyed hony & tayl hit well to gadyr with yolkes of eyron have cofyns with low bredrreys as thin as thu may draw hem put yn some stuf that the botom be helyd & let hem bake esyly & serve hem forth.

[136.] Bakyn Mete on Fisch Dayes
Take lamprons strip hem well with a lynyn cloth so that they be clene boyle hem in watyr salt venyger that they be ynow & taylle hem well in watyr & [?] salt & ley hem in the cofyn take a thike mylke of almondys drawn up with fayre watyr or with broth of fysch do to poudyr folyes of percelley salt & venyger set hem in the oven & fil hem up ther with.

[137.] A Bakyn Mete Opyn
Take the kedneys of a calfe with the swet & some dele of the flesch with all tendyr sodyn hew hit small do hit in a vessell coyle hit with creme of cow mylke sygure & good poudres & poudres of clovis safron & salt & do hit in small cofyns & bake hit as thu dedyst flathons.

[138.] A colde bakyn mete
Grynd reysons & yf thu wilte thu may boyle fegys & grynd hem ther with & temper hem up ther with sewte wyne as chargeaunt as thu may do ther to clovys macys pynes corauns datys mynsyd sygure & salt set hit on the fyre stere hit well when hit boyleth take hit of have small cofyns with low brerdys bakyn by fore & endore the brerdys with & fyll hem with safron & syryp & florych hit with anneys in confite & yf thu wilte thu may take cornels of walchnotys pike of thy skyn make hem as clene as thu may and as white he in a lytyll safron watyr set a pyn or a nedyll in hem & hold hem upryght in thy hond let not hem be to wete & ley goldfayle with that othir hond with a thyng made ther fore & blow ther on esyly with thy mouth & that shall make thy gold to a byde & so thu may gylt ovir & florich thy bakyn mete ther [f.72v] with and so thu may florich eny colde mete that ys bakyn & thu may make hit in a potage yf thu wilt that ys colde.

[139.] Caudell of Almondys
Grynd almondys blaunchyd & temper hem up with wyne or with
ale & draw hit thorow a streynour do hit in a pott & do to sigure or
hony claryfyd & safron & set hit on the fyre stere hit well as sone
as hit be gynneth to boyle take hit of & serve hit forth & yf thu wilt
cast a lytyll poudyr if gynger.

[140.] For to sle aner of foules & roste hem & serve hem forth
Cut a swan in the rofe of the mouth touward the brayn of the hede
& let hym blede to deth & kepe the blod to colour the chaudon
with or cut the necke & let hym dye then skald hym draw hym rost
hym & serve hym forth.

[141.] Crane Rostyd
Take a crane blod as thu dedyst a swan draw hym at the went fold
up hys leggys cut of his whyngys at the joynte nexte the body wend
the necke a boute the spite put the bylle yn his breste & reyse the
whinges & the legges as of a gose & yf thu shalt sauce hym mynse
hym fyrst & sauce hym with poudyr of gynger mustard & venygger
& salt & serve forth with the sauce & yf thu wilt thu may sauce
hym with sauce sylito.

[142.] Fesaunte Rostyd
Lat the fesaunt blod in the mouthe to dye pull hym drye cut a wey
the hed the nekke by body & the leggys by the kne perboyle hym
lard hym put his kneys in the vente & rost hym & res his leggys &
his wyngys as of a heyron no sauce but salt.

[143.] Pertrich Rostyd
Sle a pertrych with a feythir in the crown of the hed pul hym drye
rost hym and lard hym in the maner of a fesaunte reyse the legges
& the whynges as of a hen mynse hym sauce hym with poudyr of
gyngour & salt set hym on the fyre hete hym & set hym forth all
hote.

[144.] Quayle Rostyd
Sle a quayle lard hym rost hym as a pertyrych reyse his leggys & his
whinges as of a hene & no sauce but salt.

[145.] Heyron Rostyd
Let a heyron blode in the bouth as a crane & cut a wey the bone in the nekke & let the hed sit styll to the sknyn of the neke draw hym at the wente do hym on a spitte & wynd the skyn of the neke a boute the spitte & putt the hed yn at the golet as of a crane & breke awey the bone fro the necke to the fonte [f.73r] and lett the skyn be still & cut a wey the whyngys by the iounte nexte the body & bynd the leggys with the skyn of his legges to the spitte rost hym reys his leggys & hys whyngys as of a crane & sauce hym with poudyr of gyngour venygour & mustard & set hym forth.

[146.] Bytare Rostyd
Sle hym in the mouth as a heyron draw hym as a henne reys up his leggys as a crane let hys whyngys be on & take a wey the bone of the necke as of a heyron & putt the hedde in at the golet or in the shulder reys up his leggys & his whyngys as of a heyron & no sause but salt.

[147.] Egrett Rostyd
Dreke [break] his neke or cut the rofe of hys mouth as of a crane scall hym draw hym as a henne cut of his whyngys by the body foyle up his leggys as of a bitere rost hem reys up his leggys & his whyngys as of a heyron & no sauce butt salt.

[148.] Curlew Rostyd
Sle hym in the mouth as a crane pull hym drye cut of the whyngys by the body draw hym as a henne fold up his fete as a egrete lett his hedde & his nekke be on take a wey the nethir lipp & the thorte putt his bill in his shulder rost hym reyse his leggys & his whyngys as of a henne & no sauce but salt.

[149.] Grew Rostyd
Sle hym in the mouth as a curlew scall hym draw hym as a henne breke his leggys at the kne & take a wey the bone from the kne to the fote as an heyron & cut of the legges by the body put hym on a spitte bynd his legges as of a heyron cutt of his hedde & his neke by the body rost hym reys his leggys & his whyngys as of a heyron & no sauce but salt.

[150.] Conynggys Rostyd
Sle a conyng draw hym both a bove & by neth perbole hym lard hym rost hym take of his hedde & unlace hym sauce hym with gyngour vergeys & poudyr of gyngour.

[151.] Rabets Rostyd
Sle hym rost hym lett his hedde be on perboyle hym in fat broth rost hym unlace hym & dyghte hym as a conyng.

[152.] Sarcell Rostyd
Breke the nekke of a sarcell or of a tele pull hym drye draw hym as a chiken cut of his hedde his nekke & his whyngys & his fete rost hym [f.73v] reys his leggys & his whynggys as of a heyron & no sauce but salt.

[153.] Plover Rostyd
Breke the scolle of a plover pull hym drye sraw hym as a chiken cutt of the nekke the leggys & the whyngys by the body rost hym reyse his legges & his whynggys as of a henne & so sauce but salt.

[154.] Snyte Rostyd
Sle hym as a plover pull hym drye let his necke be hole save his whingys let the hedde be on put the hedde in his shulder fold up his legges as thu dedyst of a crane cut of the whyngys rost hym & reyse his legges & his whyngys as of a henne & no sauce but salt.

[155.] Woodcok Rostyd
Sle hym as a snyte pull hym drye or els breke his backe & kepe his scull hole draw hym as a snyte put his byll thorowgh his thyes rost hym reyse his leggys & his whyngys as of a henne & no sauce but salt.

[156.] Kyd Rostyd
Take a kyd slit the sknyn at the throte & seke the veyne in both sydes of the gorge & cut hit in two slit hit in both sydes & put both the furthir leggys & the hyndys ther yn to gedyr in both the sydes a lyttyl pryke the vont to gedyr perboyle hym lard hym serve hym forth with sauce gyngour.

[157.] Vele Rostyd

Take fayre brestys of veele perboyle ham lard hem rost hem & serve hem forth.

[158.] Venyson Rostyd

Take feyre felets cut a wey the skyn perboyle hem that they be styffe thorow lard hem with salt put hem in small brothes rost hem yf hit be nedd thu may baste hem take hem cut hem in brodd leches ley hem in dysches strew on poudyr of gyngour & salt do with buttes of venyson in the same maner & serve hem forth.

[159.] The Syde of a Dere of His Grece

Wesch hem do a wey the felets do hem on a broch scorch hem ovyr twarte & aghenne crosse wyse in the same maner of losyngys in the flesch syde rost hym take hym redde wyn poudyr of gynger poudyr of pepyr & salt & bast hit till hit be thorow have a chargeour under neth & kepe the fallyng & bast hit ther with a gene then take hit of & smyte hit as the lyst & serve hit forth.

[160.] Chikenes Farsyd

Scall chikens breke the skyne at the necke byhynd & blow hym at the skyn a ryse fro the flesch draw hem chop of the heddys wesch hem take farsure of fat porke sodyn pekyd & hewyd small with yolkes of eyron & hard yolkes cromyd small safron & salt do to gedyr & fasse youre chikens ther [f.74r] with by twyne the flesch & the skyn & blonge hem in hote broth then make hem smoth with thy the safron lye undyr the skyn then perboyle hem a lytyll & rost hem yf wilte endore hem & serve hem forth or els serve hem as they ben.

[161.] Chikenes Endoryd

Scall chykenes draw out the brest bone with thy fynggers save the flesch & the skyn hole rost hem till tham be therow then endore hem with yolkes of ayron when the endoryng ys save & hard let hem rost no more endore kydes in the same maner.

[162.] Fylets of Porke Endoryd

Rost fylets of porke endore hem with the same bature as thu dedist chikenes turnyng about on the spite & serve hem forth.

[163.] Capons of Hyee Grece Rostyd

Take a capon of hyghe grece scall hym draw hym at the vent &
draw his lyver & his gysere at the gorge & take his lef of grece &
percelley & a lytyll ysope & roosemary & a lefe or two of sage & do
hem to the grece & hew all to geder & do to hard yolkes of eyron
cromyd small & reysons of corauns good pouder saforn & salt
medyll thes to gedyr & fas with thes youre capons broch hym loike
he be stanch at the vent & at the gorge that the safron go nott out
roste hym longe with sokyng kepe the grece that falleth & base
hym ther with & kepe hym moyst till thu serve hym forth sauce
hym with gyngour as thu doist a nothir.

[164.] Capon Stewed

Take percellye sauge ysope rosemary & tyme & breke hit a lytyll
bytwyne thy hondys & stop thy capons ther with safron & couch
hem in an yryn potte yf thu have or els in a brase potte & ley
splynters coundyr neth & all a boutes by the sydes so that the
capons touch nevyr the bottom othir the sydys of the pot & strew
of the same erbys in the pott a monge the herbys be forsaydd & the
capons put a quantite & a pynt of the best vyne that thu may gete
ther to & no nothir lycour & whelme a sylver dysch a bovyn that
the breze be with yn the pott brede or els take a lede that ys made
ther for & make a bature of the white of eyron & floure & poure a
bovyn the brerdys of the ledd & stop yn with lyn cloth or papyr a
mongge the bature by twyne the sydd & the pott so that the broth
go not out loke hit be thik of bature & set the pott on charcole fyre
to the myddys of the pott and ley a quelyne on the ledd so that hit
ryse not with the hete & lete hit stew esyly & longe when thy
trouyst hit ys ynowghe take hit fro the fyre yf ys a pott of erth set
hit on a wipis of stre that hit touch nott the grownd for brekyng of
the pott & when the hete ys well [f.74v] ovir passyd take out the
capons with a pike & ley hem in a nothir vessell till thu have sey
hem that they be ynowghe and yf hit be nede couch hem in a ghen
& stop the pott a ghen & stew hem better & make a good styrip of
wyne & mynsyd datys & kanell drawyn with the same wyne &
reysons of corauns sigure safron & boyle hit a lytyll then take hit
from the fyre medyll hit with poudyr of gynger & with a lytyll of
the same wyn do ther to ley the capons on dischys & do a wey the
fat of the sewe & do the syrip to the sewe & poure a bovyn on the

capons & serve hem forth over a rib of befe & a capon to gedyr in a dysch.

[165.] Petydawe

Take garbage of yonge goose the heddys the nekkys & the whyngys the geser the hert the lyver boyle hit thorow lay hit on a bord cut the whengges & the ioutes & the feete from the leggys and eny clawe from othir cut the geser the lyver the hert in longe leches have fayre white grece fayre in a fryyng panne & cast yn all the fysch & fry hit a lytyll & put ther to poudyr of pepyr & a lytyll salt have yolkes of eyron drawyn thorow a streynour & poure yn the fryyng pan when hit ys hard a lytyll turne hit fry thorow lat nott to much but as hit may hold to gedyr & serve hit forth.

[166.] Goose or Capons Farsyd

Take percelley & swynes grece perboyle hem yn fresch broth take hem up do ther to hard yolkes hew hem to gedyr do ther to the yoys of grapys or mynsyd onyons and poudyr of gynger canell pepyr & salt & farse youre capons ther with or geese broth hem make hem stonch at the fent & at the golett so that the farsure go nott outt & rost hem up & serve hem forth.

[167.] Pygges Yfarsyd

Take porke sodyn tendyr do a wey the skyn & the bonys & hewe the flesch & half a dosyn fyggys with ale & grynd hit well to gedyr with yolkes of eyron do ther to a few reysons fryed & poudyr sigure safron & salt & yf the porke be fat do ther to gratyd bred & yf thu wilte a lytyll creme of cowmmylke & fasse the pyggys ther with but nott to full for brekyng sew the bely rost hym & serve hym forth with sauce gynger & no othir sauce.

[168.] Brestys of Motyn yn Sauce

Take brestys of motyn rostyd & chop hem take vergeys & chaf hit yn a vessell on the fyre do ther to poudyr of gynger & cast hit on the motyn choppyd.

[169.] Dyghtyng of All Maner of Fisch Trought Boyled

Take a troughte nape hym yn the hedde make the sauce of fayre watyr percelley & salt when hit be gynnyth to boyle scome hit clene draw the troughte at the bely yf thu wilt have hym rounde cut hym at the bakke yn twe placys or iij & draw hym at the thorthe nexte the hedde as thu doust a round pyke and the sauce ys vergeys serve hym cold couch on foyles of [f.75r] percelley or els sethe the pouch as thu dost the pouch of the pyke & mynse hit with g[?]y and poudyr of gynger and serve hit forth.

[170.] Crab or Lopstere
Take a crab or a lopstere stop hym at the vent with a lytyll sethe hym yn fayre watyr & no salt or els stop hym in the same maner & cast hym in the oven lat hym bake & serve hym forth cold sauce hym with venygger.

[171.] Breme yn Sauce
Shale a breme draw hym at the bely & pekke hym at the chyne bone ij or iij rost hym on a rost yron take wyne boyle hit cast ther to poudyr of gynger & vergeys & do the breme on a dysch & poure the syrip a bovyn.

[172.] Breme yn Brace
Dyght a breme in the same maner take poudyr of canell a grete dele draw hit thorow a streynour with rede wyn boyle clovys macys sygure & saundres set on the fyre when hit boyleth put ther to poudyr of gynger & venygffer & vergeys loke hit be chargeaunt of poudrys lay the breme in a chargear poure the brace a boven & serve hit forthe.

[173.] Tench yn Brace
Splay a tench by the bakke evyn thorow the hedde that the bely be hole stoch hym a lytyll ovir twarte outward in the fysch syde ley hym on a rost yron rost hym tyll he be ynowe ley hym yn a dysch the fisch syde upward take the same brace as thu dose to the breme & poure hit on & serve hit forth.

[174.] Sole yn Brace
Scle solys draw hem rost hem that they be ynowgh ley hem yn dyschys make brace as thy dost to the breme with sauce clovys macys & poudyr hit on & serve hit forth.

[175.] Storgeon
Take a storgeon cut the vyn from the tayle to the hedde & cleve

hym as a samon & cut the sydys yn fayre pecys & make the same of watyr & salt when it boyleth scome hit clene & cast the pecys ther yn & let hem boyle y nowghe then take hem up & serve hem forth with levys of percelley wete hem yn venygger cast hem in disches & the sauce ther to ys venygger.

[176.] Haddok yn Cyve

Ta Draw a haddok yn the bely yf he be large cut of the hedde & rost the body on a rost yryn till hit be ynoghe stepe brede in broth of samon or of othir god fisch draw with the broth of thyn lyvr hew percelley & do ther to a grete dele of rede wyne hole clovys macys poudyr of pepyr & a grete dele of canell & the lyver of the haddok & the pouch clene shavyn boyle hit take up the pouch & the lyver & do hit to gadyr hewyn small yn a pott & reysons of corauns safron & saunders & salt boyle hit & sesyn hit up with pouder of gynger [f.75v] and vergeys do a wey the skyn of the haddok lay hym on a chargeour poure the gyve a bovyn and serve hit forth.

[177.] Soupes Chamlayn

Take wyne canell poudyr of gynger & sigure of eche a porcon stamp hit a while to gedyr hong a streynour ovir a vessell let hit hong stillk ij or iij hourys take payndemayn & cut yn maner of brewys tost hem ovyr both sydys & cast on blaunch poudyr & the syrip abovyn & serve hit forth.

[178.] Coddlyng Leng Haddoke & Hake

Draw hem by the bely cut hem ovir twarte yn round pecys yf the haddok be large cut of the hedde & make a longe tayle to serve make thy sauce of watyr & salt when hit boyleth scome hit clene & cast yn the lyver & the fysch & thy percelley & let hit stond in the sauce till you serve then serve hit forth hote & the lyver ther withe & sauce hit with garkeck stp the haddok & serv hym coldd & serve hem with sauce gynger.

[179.] Bace Mylet or Breme

Draw all thes at the bely scale hem clene with the ege of a knyf wesch hym make thy sauce of watyr & salt when hit boyleth scome hit clene & schorch fyrst othyr twarte to the syde & cast hit yn the wellyng sayce sage & percelley & serve hit forth somdell hote serve the base & the melet with sauce gynger & the breme with garlecke.

[180.] Congur Turbutt Halibut Poyled
Scale a congur nott yn hott watyr for brestyng of the hedde & yf thu wylt thu may cleve hym cut thy congur a lytyll by fore the navyll by the bely that thu may louse the gutte take hit out at the thorte & the lyver at the gutte & the draght cut all the bely ovir thwarte yn round pecys loke thy hore be shavyn a wey fro the bakke & of the bely to the tayle & all the fysch shall be shavyn clene so that the skyn be nott a wey & hit be ryght white draw thy turbut by the wyn by neth the gill & cut of the hedde & the white sydd fro the blacke & gedyr of thy gyll with a knyfe on both sydes yf thy turbut be large clene doun ryght enlong & yf he be lytill cut hym ovyr twharte & enddlong thy rybbys chyne & all thy halibut cut yn the same maner & cast hit fayre watyr & kepe hit white make thy sauce of fayre watyr and yf thu do eny salt ther to let hit be but a lytyll when hit boyleth scome hit clene when the congur ys y now take hit up with a scomer & ley hit yn a vessell with fayre watyr & salt & have fayr watyr & salt yn an othir vessell & when the turbut & thy halybutt ys boyled poure out the broth & put yn a lytyll cold watyr & salt upon the fysch with thy hond for brekyng & ley hit yn watyr & salt & serve congure ij or iij pecys on a chargeor for thy sovaynys & strew on foyles of percelley & serve the remnaunt for othir men & sauce hit with vergeys & of the turbut or of the halybut ley on or two of the broddyse yn a chargeour & sauce hit with verge sauce & strew on foyles of percelley. [f.76r]

[181.] Gurnarde or Roch Boyled
Draw hem by the syde from the fyn dounward & save thy sounde & thy resete with thyn slyt hem the poke & the shave hit clene & let hit hong by & wesch hem & make sauce of watyr & salt when hit boyleth scome hit clene & cast yn the fysch when hit ys boyled thorow take hit up esyly with a scomer & let hit dry & serve hit forth cold & sauce hit with sauce gynger.

[182.] Playce Solys and Flounderres Boyled
Draw thy playce undyr the fyn cut of thy hedde by the gyll clen hym aftyr the shulders along aftyr the chyn on the white syde ale a sole draw hym byneth the gyll & let the hedde be on draw a

52

flounder on the bakke syde undyr the fyn ovir thwarte the brest &
seynt andrew ys crosse in the white syde wesch hym clene make thy
sauce of fayre watyr & salt & when hit boyleth scome hit clene &
cast yn thy fisch cast ther to percelley & ale scome hit & serve hit
forth hote & the flounders yn the same sauce & the foyle dry yn
white wyn or ale & poudyr of gynger & mustard.

[183.] Welkes Boyled
Do welkes yn a pott with watyr so that they may flete ther yn set
hem on a esy fyre let hem seth sokyngly & long then take hem up
& poure a wey the watyr & pyke the fisch out of the shill with a
pikke & take of the hatte fro the hedde so hem on a vessell with a
lytyll cold watyr so that they be unnethe helyd & a grete dele of salt
& scoure the welkes well with thyn hond let all the slyme goo of &
wesch hem yn othir iiij waters & ley hem yn othir clene water till
thu serve hem forth then do hem a brode yn dysches & strew on
fayles of percelley.

[184.] Perch Boyled
Draw a perche at the gyll lett the bely be hole make a styfe sauce of
watyr & salt & yf thu wilt thu may put to ale when hit boyleth
scome hit clene & cast yn the perch & let hym boyle well then strip
the skyn on both sydys & let the gedde be on and the tayle then ley
hym on disches & strew on foyles of percelley serve forth cold &
serve hym with venygger.

[185.] Fresch Makrell Boyled
Draw a makrell at the gyll save the bely hole wesch hit make thy
sauce of watyr & salt when hit boyleth cast yn percelley & croppys
of mynttys & do yn thy fysch ther to & serve hit forth hote &
sauce hit with vergeys.

[186.] Shrympys Boyled
Take quyke shrympys pike hem clene make thy sauce of watyr &
salt cast hem yn let hem boyle but a lytyll poure a wey the watyr ley
hem [f.76v] dry when thu shalt serve hem forth ley hem yn disches
round all aboughte the sydes of the disches & ley the backesyde
outward & eny course till ye come to the mydward of the disches
with in eerve hem forth sauce hem with venygger.

[187.] Soupys yn Dorye

Blaunch almound grynd hem & tempyr hem up with watyr yn to a good mylke drawyn thorow a streynour yn to a pott put to safron & yf thu wilte thu may colour hit a lytyll therwith & put to sygure & salt sett hit on the fyre stere hit & when hit ys at boylyng do yn a lytyll good wyne take hit fro the fyre stere hit alway fro quellyng have white bredde cut yn shyvys as brues take & tost hit a lytyll on a rost yron that hit be somdell broun dip hit a lytyll on the wyn & ley hit a lytyll aghen on the rost yron & tost hit & do to a lytyll mylke yn disches & couch iij or iiij shyvys yn a dysch & poure on the mylke a bovyn & serve hit forth hote.

[188.] Hote Mylke of Almoundys

Blaunch almoundys grynd hem tempyr hem up with fayre watyr do to sygure or hony claryfyd sett hit on the fyre steyr hit well when hit boyleth serve hit forth hote & bredd tostyd yn othir dysches.

[189.] Cold Mylke of Almondys

Do fayre watyr yn a pott do ther to blaunch sigure or blake sigure or hony claryfyd so that hit be somdell doucet & do a lytyll salt ther to set hit on the fyre when hit ys at boylyng scome hit clene lett hit boyle wekk then take hit of & lett hit kele then blaunch almondys grynd hem & temper hem up with the same watyr yn to a thyke mylke & poure ther to a lytyll wyn that hit have a lytyll sa safyr ther of then cut brede yn shyvs & tost hem on a tost yron that they be somdell brown then bast hem a lytlyll with wyn & ley hem on aghen till they be hard & serve hem forth yn anothir disch with the mylke.

NOTES ON THE RECIPES

1. (untitled recipe)

The first recipe in the manuscript isn't listed in the table of contents, probably because of its lack of title. While there are many cabbage (cole) recipes in the medieval corpus, there are two that seem to be related to this one.

The first is a recipe for "Worts" that is a parallel of recipe 142 in *A Noble Book off Cookry*.

> To mak wortes tak coles and stripe them from the stalks then tak betees avens borage violettes mallowes parsly betayne prymrose pacyens the whyt of lekes and cropes of nettilles and parboile them upon a bord and pres out the water and mynce them smalle put ther to otemelle and tak the brothe of turbot congur samon or other fisshe and put them in a pot with the for said erbes and when the pot is at boillinge call in the erbes and the wort and boile them up and salt them and ye tak brothe tak eles and boile them and tak them upe and strip the fisshe from the bones and grind it up with the sam brothe and put them all to the wort and sethe them up. Also ye may sethe muskelles with as mych water as they may swym in and boile them tille they be opyne then streyne the brothe and tak some erbes as ye did befor and put it to the muskall brothe and set them on the fyere and boile them and when they be boiled put to the erbes and the brothe and put to the drawen muskalls

and salt them, and ye may tak pessen drawe through a streyn and mak them up with the wort and faire water and put ther to oile that hath bene skald and in the boiling alay it up with pessene ye shall put none otemele ther in, also parboile the whit of lekes and pres out the water and chop them smalle and canebyns with faire water and set it to the fyere to boile it and put yt to the whit of leekes but do none otemele ther in and salt it and serue it. [A Noble Boke off Cookry (England, 1468)]

Near the end they both include (twice!) one of my favorite bits in medieval recipes - an instruction not to add any oatmeal. Odd, considering the recipe clearly calls for oatmeal early on. Oats must have been a common addition to cooked cabbage, as I've found this instruction in other similar recipes that otherwise didn't mention them.

This recipe also seems to be connected to this one for "Joutes" in *Liber cure cocorum* that the list of ingredients at the start is similar.

For Ioutes. Take most of cole, borage, persyl, Of plumtre leves, þou take þer tyl, Redde nettel crop and malues grene, Rede brere croppes, and avans goode, A lytel nept violet by þo rode, And lest of prymrol levus þou take, Sethe hom in water for goddes sake. Þenne take hom up, presse oute þou shalle Þe water, and hakke þese erbs alle And grynd hom in a morter schene With grotene. and sethe hom thyk by dene In fresshe brothe, as I þe kenne. Take sklyset, enbawdet þenne Besyde on platere þou shalt hit lay To be cut and eten with ioutes in fay. [Liber cure cocorum, (England, 1430)]

2. For to make canabenes
This recipe shows some of the problems with transcribing a handwritten manuscript. There are words here that are unclear, and it could be a problem with spelling, with my reading or with the scribe who wrote it in the first place.

Using a parallel recipe, number 143 from *A Noble Boke off Cookry* makes it a bit clearer.

To mak canebyns tak whit benes and lay them to stepe in rynynge water ij dais and ij nights and change the water eury day then tak them up and let them are and put them in an ovene to hardyne and shelle them at the mylne and put away the hulles and clef the benes in ij or iiij or iiiij at the most and fry them and ye may kep them as longe as ye will. [A Noble Boke off Cookry (England, 1468)]

The word "tjylle" is most likely meant to be "mill", and "evehys" to be "hulls", but no matter how I look at the script I can't get the letters to resolve that way.

3. Canabens
This short little recipe is clearly a parallel of recipe 144 in *A Noble Boke off Cookry*.

To mak another canebyns take canebines and wesshe them and step them a litille and mak them up with mylk of almondes put ther to sugur and salt, and out of lent mak it up with mylk and clarified hony then salt it and serue it. [A Noble Boke off Cookry (England, 1468)]

The use of honey in *A Noble Boke off Cookry* instead of sugar is interesting given that sugar's place in English cooking was pretty well established by the fifteenth century. The *Wagstaff* version adds some butter, but the recipes are essentially the same.

4. Canabens With Bacone
This recipe parallels number 145 in *A Noble Boke off Cookry*.

To mak canebyns with bacon tak and put swete brothe in a pot then wesche canebyns clene and put to none other licour but boile them up and let them be salt and serue them then tak ribbes of bacon boled and do away the skyn and lay them in another disshe and serue them as ye do furmente and venysen. [A Noble Boke off Cookry (England, 1468)]

The only significant difference is that in the version from *A Noble Boke off Cookry*, the recipe refers to frumenty, but *Wagstaff* only mentions venison in broth.

While not directly related, there's a similar recipe in *Forme of Cury*.

> For To Make Gronden Benes. I. Take benes and dry hem in a nost or in an Ovene and hulle hem wele and wyndewe out þe hulk and wayshe hem clene an do hem toseeþ in gode broth an ete hem with Bacon. [Forme of Cury (England, 1390)]

All told, I've found six different recipes in medieval cookbooks for beans with bacon. It was obviously a popular combination that is still common in the modern day.

5. Butturde Wortys

As with the previous recipes, this one has a parallels in number 146 from *A Noble Boke off Cookry*.

> To mak buttered wortes tak good erbes and pik them and wesche them and shred them and boile them in watur put ther to clarified buttur a good quantite and when they be boiled salt them and let none otemele cum ther in then cutt whit bred thyn in dysshes and pour on the wort. [A Noble Boke off Cookry (England, 1468)]

As I mentioned in the note on the first recipe above, this one includes the admonition "let none otemele come there yne" even though there is no previous mention of oatmeal in the recipe. This suggests that oatmeal was typically added to cooked greens.

This recipe shows up in other sources as well.

> To make buttyrd Wortys. Take all maner of gode herbys that ye may gette pyke them washe them and hacke them and boyle them vp in fayre water and put ther to butture clarefied A grete quantite And when they be boylde enowgh salt them but let non Ote mele come ther yn And dyse brede in small gobbetts

& do hit in dyshys and powre the wortes A pon and serue hit furth. [MS Pepys 1047 (England, ca. 1500)]

Buttered Wortes. Take al maner of good herbes that thou may gete, and do bi ham as is forsaid; putte hem on the fire with faire water; put there-to clarefied buttur a grete quantite. Whan thei ben boyled ynogh, salt hem; late none otemele come there-in. Dise brede small in disshes, and powre on the wortes, and serue hem forth. [Two Fifteenth-Century Cookery-Books (England, 1430)]

6. Cabogys
As expected, this recipe parallels number 146 from *A Noble Boke off Cookry.*

To mak cabages wortis tak whit cabage and fined them smale and mak them up, also tak whit cabages and cut them from the stalks and wesche them and parboile them and presse out the water and hew them smale in flesshe tym put fat brothe of beef in a pot of capon brothe or the brothe of other good flesche and when it is boiled put in thy cabages and maribones all to brokene and boile them up do ther to saffron or salt and alay it upe with grond bred and luk it be chargant of canebyns and serue it. [A Noble Boke off Cookry (England, 1468)]

There are a couple of interesting differences. The first part from *Noble* ("To mak cabages wortis tak whit cabage and fined them smale and mak them up"), seems redundant and doesn't appear in the *Wagstaff* version. Perhaps it was a copyist error. *Noble* also has the added instruction at the end to make sure the recipe is either as thick as canebeans, or is thick with canebeans.

7. Hare or goose powdryde in Wortys
This is the first recipe that isn't centered around cabbage or beans, though it does call for both cabbage and oatmeal. This recipe parallels number 148 in *A Noble Boke off Cookry.*

To mak hayre or goose poudred in wort put good brothe of flesshe in a pot and maribones and set it on the fyere and chope the haire in peces, and put ther to and draw the brothe throughe a streyn with the blod then tak coles the whit of leekes other erbes and otemele and shred them smale to gedur and it be an old hayre let hir boile welle or ye put in your wortis and it be a younge hayre put in the hare and the wort to gedure and els tak a goos of a nyght and a day murdring and chope hir in the wort in the sam manner and serue it. [A Noble Boke off Cookry (England, 1468)]

There is also a similar recipe in *Two Fifteenth-Century Cookery-Books*.

Hare in Wortes. Take Colys, and stripe hem faire fro the stalkes. Take Betus and Borage, auens [correction; sic = MS. anens.] , Violette, Malvis, parsle, betayn, pacience, the white of the lekes, and the croppe of the netle; parboile, presse out the water, hew hem small, And do there-to mele. Take goode broth of ffressh beef, or other goode flessh and mary bones; do it in a potte, set on the fire; choppe the hare in peces, And, if thou wil, wassh hir in the same broth, and then drawe it thorgh A streynour with the blode, And then put all on the fire. And if she be an olde hare, lete hire boile well, or thou cast in thi wortes; if she be yonge, cast in all togidre at ones; And lete hem boyle til thei be ynogh, and ceson hem with salt. And serue hem forth. The same wise thou may make wortes of A Gose of a niȝt, powdryng of beef, or eny other fressh flessh. [Two Fifteenth-Century Cookery-Books (England, 1430)]

The word "powdered" here means salted (i.e. covered in powdered salt), and apparently only applies to the goose. Interesting that the version in *Two Fifteenth-Century Cookery-Books* specifies that the goose is only to be salted for one night, and that the *Wagstaff* recipe doesn't mention salting the goose at all.

8. Joutys yne flesch days
This recipe reads like an expanded version of one from *Ancient Cookery*.

Joutes on flesh day. Take cole, and borage, and lang de beefs (buglofs), and parsell, and betes, and arage, and avence, and vyolet, and saveray, and fenelle, and sethe hom; and when thei ben sothen, (boiled) take and preffe oute clene the watur, and hewe hom smalle, and do hom in a pot, and put thereto gode brothe, and let hit sethe, and serve hit forthe.   [Arundel 334 (England, 1425)]

9. Lentyn foyles

I haven't found any clear parallels to this recipe. The combination of herbs, onions, raisins, and almond milk is very unusual.

10. Longe wortys

While this recipe references the previous ones for varied leafy plants (coles/worts), it also calls for peas. There are recipes with similar names in *Two Fifteenth-Century Cookery-Books*, one for peas and the other for just the worts, but neither is a close match.

Lange Wortys de chare. Take beeff and merybonys, and boyle yt in fayre water; than take fayre wortys and wassche hem clene in water, and parboyle hem in clene water; than take hem vp of the water after the fyrst boylyng, an cut the leuys a-to or a-thre, and caste hem in-to the beff, and boyle to gederys: than take a lof of whyte brede and grate yt, an caste it on the pot, an safron and salt, and let it boyle y-now, and serue forth. [Two Fifteenth-Century Cookery-Books (England, 1430)]

Longe Wortes de Pesone. Take grene pesyn, and wassh hem clene, And cast hem in a potte, and boyle hem til they breke; and then take hem vppe fro the fire, and putte hem in the broth in an other vessell; And lete hem kele; And drawe hem thorgh a Streynour into a faire potte. And then take oynones in ij. or iiij. peces; And take hole wortes, and boyle hem in fayre water; And then take hem vppe, And ley hem on the faire borde, And kutte hem in .iij. or in .iiij. peces; And caste hem and the oynons into that potte with the drawen pesen, and late hem boile togidre til they be all tendur, And then take faire oile and fray, or elle3 fressh broth of some maner fissh, (if thou maist, oyle a quantite), And caste thereto saffron, and salt a quantite. And lete hem boyle wel togidre til they ben ynogh; and stere hem well euermore, And serue hem forthe. [Two Fifteenth-Century Cookery-Books (England, 1430)]

There is a similar recipe however in *Forme of Cury*.

Frenche. XX.III. XIII. Take and seeþ white peson and take oute þe perrey & parboile erbis & hewe hem grete & caft hem in a pot with the perrey pulle oynouns & seeþ hem hole wel in water & do hem to þe Perrey with oile & salt, colour it with safroun & messe it and cast þeron powdour douce. [Forme of Cury (England, 1390)]

11. Blaunche pore

There are many recipes for "Blaunche Porre" in medieval cookbooks, suggesting that it was a popular dish. The following are some that are close to the one above.

Blaunche porre. Take the clene white of lekes wel wasshed, and sethe hom; and when thai byn sothen, draw oute the grene pith, that is within, and then preffe oute the water, and hak hom smal, and bray hom; and in the brayinge alay hit with thik almonde mylk; and then sethe hit, and cast therto sugre, and make hit sumqwat rennynge (rather thin) ; and when hit is sothen and dressed up in dilfches, then cast suger above, and serve hit forthe. [Arundel 334, (England, 1425)]

Take the qwyte (white) of lekes and parboyle hom, and hew hom small, and take onyons and mynse hom therewith, and do hom in a pot, and put thereto gode broth, broth, and let hit boyle, and do therto smale briddes (birds), and scth hom therewyth, and colour hit wyth saffron, and do therto pouder marchantf, and serve hit forthe. [Arundel 334, (England, 1425)]

Blanche porrey. Take blanche almondes, And grinde hem, and drawe hem with sugur water thorgh a streynour into a good stuff mylke into a potte; and then take the white of lekes, and

hew hem small, and grynde hem in a morter with brede; and
then cast al to the mylke into the potte, and caste therto sugur
and salt, and lete boyle; And seth feyre poudrid eles in faire
water ynowe, and broile hem on a gredren; and kut hem in
faire longe peces, and ley two or thre in a dissh togidre as ye do
veneson with ffurmenty, And serue it forthe. [Two Fifteenth-
Century Cookery-Books (England, 1430)]

For to make Blawnche Perrye. Take the Whyte of the lekys, an
sethe hem in a potte, an presse hem vp, and hacke hem smal
on a bord. An nym gode Almaunde Mylke, an a lytil of Rys, an
do alle thes to-gederys, an sethe an stere it wyl, an do ther-to
Sugre or hony, an dresse it yn; thanne take powderd Elys, an
sethe hem in fayre Water, and broyle hem, an kytte hem in
long pecys. And ley .ij. or .iiij. in a dysshe, and putte thin (Note:
Thine.) perrey in a-nother dysshe, an serue the to dysshys to-
gederys as Venysoun with Furmenty. [Two Fifteenth-Century
Cookery-Books (England, 1430)]

12. Pome perre

This is another odd recipe with no clear parallels in other medieval
English cookbooks. The closest thing I could find is a French
recipe for "White Bruet" from *Du fait de cuisine*.

23. And first, for your white bruet take almonds according to
the quantity of the potage which you are told to make, and
have them blanched and cleaned and brayed cleanly, and
moisten them with the purée of white peas; and when they are
well brayed draw them up with the said broth of peas and put
it in according to the quantity of the said almonds; and put in
good white wine and verjuice and white ginger and grains of
paradise, and everything in measure, and salt, and check that
you have not put in too much of anything; and put sugar in
according to the quantity of the broth; and then take a fair,
large, clear and clean pot and put to boil. And when this is at
the sideboard put your fried fish on fair serving dishes and
then throw the said bruet on top; and on the potages which
you make from almonds from here on, when it is to be dressed

do not forget the sugar-spice pellets [dragiees] which should be scattered on top. [Du fait de cuisine (France, 1420)]

13. Gingaudre

There are several recipes for "Gingawdry" in medieval English cookbooks, but none that are precisely the same. For example, this is the only one of them that specifically calls for only hake, with the others listing a variety of fish. Here are a couple of them.

> Gyngawdry. XX.IIII. XIIII. Take the Powche and the Lyuour of haddok, codlyng and hake and of ooþer fisshe, parboile hem, take hem and dyce hem small, take of the self broth and wyne, a layour of brede of galyntyne with gode powdours and salt, cast þat fysshe þerinne and boile it. & do þerto amydoun. & colour it grene. [Forme of Cury (England, 1390)]

> Gyngawtre. Take the pake (a quantity) of the lyver of hake, or of codlynge, or of hadok, and parboyle hit well; then take hit up and dyse hit smal (cut it small as dice); and do hit in a postenet, and do therto the fatte of the brothe and wyn, and take light bred, and drawe hit up with the brothe nentz to thik (not too thick); and do therto galentyne a lytel, and pouder of clowes, and of maces, and let hit boyle, and colour hit grene, and serve hit forthe. [Arundel 334 (England, 1425)]

I suspect the word "pake" in the Arundel 334 version is actually supposed to be "poke" (e.g. pouch or sack).

The name of the recipe, along with instructions in some of the recipes to color it with parsley, show a connection to the word "gaudy," which in Middle English was the name of a particular shade of green.

14. Eles yne sorre

Below are three recipes for "Eels in Sorre" from medieval English cookbooks, all of which are similar to the one above.

Eles in sorry. Take eles and cut hom on culpons, and wassh hom, and take a potte, and do therin faire watur, and a lytell wyne and onyons mynced, and gode herbes, and let hit sethe; then do thi fysshe therto, and pouder of ginger and of canell, and colour hit withe faunders, and serve hit forthe. [Arundel 334 (England, 1425)]

Eles in surre. Take eles culponde (cut in pieces) and clene wafshen, and sethe hom with half wyne, half water; arid cast therto onyons mynced, clowes, maces, pynes, railinges of corance ; and draw up a Hour therto of chippes of bred steped in wyne ; then carte therto pouder of pepur, and afterward the Hour, and also saunders and saffron; and in the scttynge doune put therto pouder of ginger, and of canel medelet with a lytel vinegur, and serve hit forthe. [Arundel 334 (England, 1425)]

Elys in Sorre. Take eles, and fle hem, and choppe hem in faire colpons, And wassh hem clene, and putte hem in a faire potte; and then take parcelly, oynons, and shrede togidre to the eles; And then take pouder of peper, and broth of fissh, and set hit ouer the fire, and lete hem boyle togidre; And then take a lofe of brede, and alay the brede in the the same broth, And drawe hit thorgh a streynour; And whan the eles ben almoost y-sodde ynowe, caste there-to; And lete hem boile togidre; and take hem vp fro the fire, and cast ther-to salte, vinegre, And serue hit forth. [Two Fifteenth-Century Cookery-Books (England, 1430)]

Additionally, there are a couple of other eel recipes that seem very close.

To mak eles in bruet tak eles culpond and boile them with mynced onyons padley and saige and draw it with whit bred and wyne put ther to pouder of pepper canelle and salt and serue it. [A Noble Boke off Cookry (England, 1468)]

Cvij - Sore Sengle. Take Elys or Gurnard, and parte hem half in Wyne, and half in watere, in-to a potte; take Percely and Oynonys and hewe hem smalle; take Clowes or Maces and

65

caste ther-on; take Safroun, and caste ther-to, and sette on the fyre, and let boyle tylle it be y-now; then sette it a-doun; take poudere Gyngere, Canelle, Galyngale, and temper it vppe with Wyne, and cast on the potte and serue forth. [Two Fifteenth-Century Cookery-Books (England, 1430)]

15. Pykes or elys in ballocbrothe

This recipe is a clear parallel to number 149 in *A Noble Boke off Cookry.*

Pik and eles in ballok brothe / that muste our dame haue, or / els she will be wrothe. To mak eles and pikes in ballok brothe tak and splat a pik and splat hym and skale hym and culpon eles smale and put them in a pot do ther to grene onyons and quybibes and mynce them and sesson them up with a liore of bred and put it to clowes maces pouder of canelle and saffron and put ther to a quantite of stok fische lik unto the eles and let the pik boile esely and serue the hole pik for a lord and quarto of a pik for comons and culpans and let them be sessoned and put the brothe with the sauce upon the pyk and serve it. [A Noble Boke off Cookry (England, 1468)]

16. Frumente yne lentyne

This recipe is a clear parallel of number 150 in *A Noble Boke off Cookry.*

To make furmente with porpas in lent tak clene whet and bet it in a mortoire and vane it clene and sethe it till it be on enbreston then tak blanched almondes and grind them in a mortoire and drawe ther of swet mylk with the brothe and boile it till it be tendur and colour it with saffron and leshe thy porpas and when it is sodene lay it in dishes and serue it furthe in dysshes. [A Noble Boke off Cookry (England, 1468)]

The one odd point is that in the half-dozen or so similar recipes scattered throughout the existing medival English cookbooks, this appears to be the only version that does not refer to porpoise in the title.

17. Pylets yne sarcene

This recipe is similar to the recipe below for "Pompys" - essentially meatballs in an almond milk based sauce.

> Pompys. Take Beef, Porke, or Vele, on of hem, and raw, alle to-choppe it atte the dressoure, than grynd hem in a morter as smal as thou may, than caste ther-to Raw 3olkys of Eyroun, wyn, an a lytil whyte sugre: caste also ther-to pouder Pepyr, and Macys, Clowes, Quybibys, pouder Canelle, Synamoun, and Salt, and a lytil Safroun; then take and make smale Pelettys round y-now, and loke that thou haue a fayre potte of Freysshe brothe of bef or of Capoun, and euer throw hem ther-on and lete hem sethe tyl that they ben y-now; then take and draw vppe a thryfty mylke of Almaundys, with cold freysshe brothe of Bef, Vele, Moton, other Capoun, and a-lye it with floure of Rys and with Spycerye; and atte the dressoure ley thes pelettys .v. or .vj. in a dysshe, and then pore thin sewe aneward, and serue in, or ellys make a gode thryfty Syryppe and ley thin pelettys atte the dressoure ther-on, and that is gode seruyse. [Two Fifteenth-Century Cookery-Books (England, 1430)]

The word "sarcene" in the recipe refers to the dark red color of the sauce, which may be connected to a belief at the time that Saracens had dark red skin.

18. To make Jussalle

This recipe is a reasonably clear match to recipe 151 in *A Noble Boke off Cookry*.

> To mak jusselle tak the swet brothe of a capon or of other good flesshe and set it on the fyere in a large vesselle colour it with saffron put ther to saige cut gret and salt it then tak eggs and drawe them through a strener and temper grated bread and eggs and stirre it to gedure till they be ronn and let the erbes be well mellid to gedur and when yt begynnythe to boille tak out the pot stik and turn the curd about with a scorner and let not the fyere be to hasty when it is throughe knyt tak it from the fyere and couyr it and serue it. [A Noble Boke off Cookry (England, 1468)]

Recipes for "jussel" show up in just about every medieval English cookbook, with some variants having instructions for meatless days or specifying the use of other broths. The closest of these is probably the following one from *Two Fifteenth-Century Cookery-Books*.

> Guissell. Take faire capon broth, or of beef, And sette hit ouer the fire, and caste therto myced sauge, parcelly and saffron, And lete boile; And streyn the white and the yolke of egges thorgh a streynour, and caste there-to faire grated brede, and medle hit togidre with thi honde, And caste the stuff to the broth into the pan; And stirre it faire and softe til hit come togidre, and crudded; And then serue it forth hote. [Two Fifteenth-Century Cookery-Books, (England, 1430)]

19. To make leche lardys of iij colours

The trick of producing a dish in a variety of different colors seems to have been popular throughout medieval Europe, with many recipes such as blancmanger or jelly appearing in surviving cookbooks with instructions for how to color them.

While there are no exact parallels to this recipe for larded milk of three colors, the two below are good examples of recipes that are very similar.

> Lete Lardes. XX.III. VIII. Take parsel and grynde with a Cowe mylk, medle it with ayrenn and lard ydyced take mylke after þat þou hast to done and myng þerwith. and make þerof dyuerse colours. If þou wolt have zelow, do þerto safroun and no parsel. If þou wolt have it white; nonþer parsel ne safroun but do þerto amydoun. If þou wilt have rede do þerto sandres. If þou wilt have pownas do þerto turnesole. If þou wilt have blak do þerto blode ysode and fryed. and set on the fyre in as many vessels as þou hast colours þerto and seeþ it wel and lay þise colours in a cloth first oon. and sithen anoþer upon him. and sithen the þridde and the ferthe. and presse it harde til it be all out clene. And whan it is al colde, lesh it thynne, put it in a panne and fry it wel. and serue it forth. [Forme of Cury (England, 1390)]

Letlardes. Take mylke scalding hote; And take eyren, the yolkes and the white, and drawe hem thorgh a streynour, and caste to the mylke; And then drawe the iuce of herbes, which that thou will, so that they ben goode, and drawe hem thorgh a streynour. And whan the mylke bigynneth to crudde, caste the Iuce thereto, if thou wilt haue it grene; And if thou wilt haue it rede, take Saundres, and cast to the mylke whan it croddeth, and leue the herbes; And if thou wilt haue hit yelowe, take Saffron, and caste to the mylke whan hit cruddeth, and leve the Saundres; And if thou wilt haue it of al thes colours, take a potte with mylke and Iuse of herbes, and another potte with mylke and saffron; And another potte with mylke and saundres, and put hem al in a lynnen clothe, and presse hem al togidur; And if thou wilt haue it of one colour, take but one cloth, (Note: Douce MS. of these) and streyne it in a cloth in the same maner, and bete on the clothe with a ladell or a Skymour, to make sad or (Note: Douce MS. and.) flatte; and leche it faire with a knyfe, and fry the leches in a pan with a litull fressh grece; And take a litull, and put hit in a dissh, and serue it forth. [Two Fifteenth-Century Cookery-Books (England, 1430)]

The word "leche" in the *Wagstaff* recipe means "slice", which suggests that the final product is something thick and solid enough to be sliced. In the other versions of this recipe it is given as "lete", which is a corruption of the French "lait" (milk). It's possible that somewhere in the copying of recipes from one text to another, "lete" was accidentally misunderstood as "leche".

20. To make umbelys of a dere
This appears to be the only surviving recipe for deer kidneys that specifies that they are to be used "blood and all". The similar recipes for "umbles", "humbles", and "numbles" from other medieval cookbooks either do not make any reference to blood, or specifically call for the blood to be pressed out.

One possibility is hinted at in a recipe from *A Noble Boke off Cookry*.

To mak nombles tak hert middrif and kidney and hew them smalle and prise out the blod and sethe them in water and ale and colour it with brown bred or with blod and fors it with canell and galingalle and when it boilithe kole it a litille with ale and serwe it. [A Noble Boke off Cookry (England, 1468)]

Here blood is being added back into the recipe for color, so it may be that the *Wagstaff* version leaves the blood in the kidneys so that the final product will be dark red or black.

21. Grewel enforsede
This recipe is very close to recipe 153 in *A Noble Boke off Cookry*, with the only notable difference being that the *Wagstaff* recipe adds saffron along with an extra boiling step at the end.

To mak grewelle enforced tak mary bones and freche brothe and mak grewelle and draw them throughe a strener then tak pork sodene tender and pick out the bones and the senewes and pille of the skyn and hew it and grind it smale in a mortair and temper it with the same gruelle that is drawen and mak it smothe and let it stond myche by freche pork and salt it and serue it. [A Noble Boke off Cookry (England, 1468)]

Interestingly, both of those aspects missing in *Noble* are present in the version from Liber Cure Cocorum, though the wording is very different.

For gruel of fors. Fyrst take porke, wele þou hit sethe With otene grotes, þat ben so smethe. Whenne hit begynnes wele to alye, þou save of þe þynnest brothe þer by To streyne þy gruel, alle and summe. But furst take oute þy porke þou mun And hak hit smal and grynde hit clene. Cast hit to þo gruel þat streyned bene, Colour hit with safroune and sethe hit wele. For gruel of force serve hom at mele. [Liber cure cocorum, (England, 1430)]

22. Chaudone of Salmone

This recipe is a clear parallel of recipe 154 in *A Noble Boke off Cookry*.

> To mak chaudron for samone tak the draught of samon and mak it clene and put it in a pot and all the blod of the samon ther with and boile it till it be enoughe then tak it up and grind the spawn and draw a liour of bred and of whit wyne and put ther to poudere of pepper and canelle and boile it and stirr it and sesson it up with pouder of guinger venygar saffron and salt and ye may serve it furthe in sted of potage or els a sauce for samon. [A Noble Boke off Cookry (England, 1468)]

There is also a close match in *Two Fifteenth-Century Cookery-Books*, and a similar recipe in Forme of Cury.

> Chaudewyne. Take the Guttes of fressh Samon, and do awey the gall; and slytte hem, and caste hem in a potte, and boyle hem in water right well; And ley hem vpon a borde, and hewe hem; And then stepe brede in the same licour, And cast som of the samon broth thereto, And drawe all thorgh a streynour; and then caste the hewen guttes and the drawen brede in a potte, and a litull wyn, pouder of Canell, or saffron, And lete boyle togidre; And cast there-to pouder of peper, Vinegre, and salt; And lete hit be rennyng. [Two Fifteenth-Century Cookery-Books (England, 1430)]

> CAWDEL OF SAMOUN C.XI. Take the guttes of Samoun and make hem clene. perboile hem a lytell. take hem up and dyce hem. slyt the white of Lekes and kerue hem smale. cole the broth and do the lekes þerinne with oile and lat it boile togyd yfere. do the Samoun icorne þerin, make a lyour of Almaundes mylke & of brede & cast þerto spices, safroun and salt, seeþ it wel. and loke þat it be not stondyng. [Forme of Cury (England, 1390)]

All of these recipes appear to be fish-day versions of a sort of stew or sauce made from the offal of swans.

Chaudoun. Take gysers, and lyuers, and hert of Swanne; and if the guttys ben fat, slyt them clence thaym, and caste them ther-to, and boile them in faire watre: and thanne take them up, and hew them smal, and thanne caste them in-to the same brothe, (but strayne hit thurgh a straynour firste); and caste ther-to poudre peper, canel, and vynegre, and salt, and lete boile. And thanne take the blode of the Swanne, and freysshe broth, and brede, and draw them thurwe a straynour, and cast ther-to; and lete boile to-gedre. And thenne take poudre of gyngere, whanne hit is al-moste y-now, and put ther-to, and serue forth with the swan.   [Two Fifteenth-Century Cookery-Books (England, 1430)]

23. Cokkes of kellynge
This recipe is very similar to recipe 155 in *A Noble Boke off Cookry*, with the differences being either minor changes in wording or possibly copying errors.

To dight codlinge or keling tak a kelinge and cut them smale and put them in brothe of freche samon and boile them put ther to almond mylk and drawe bred and colour them with saffon and sanders do ther to sugur and pouder of pepper and serue it and other fisshe among as turbot pike samon chopped and sesson them with venygur and salt it and serue it.   [A Noble Boke off Cookry (England, 1468)]

The word "cokkes" in *Wagstaff* is most certainly supposed to be "coddes", and "kellynge" (keling) is defined by Mayhew and Skeat as "a large kind of cod". The use of milk in *Wagstaff* is a clear departure from what would otherwise be a recipe for a fish day, and is likely an error since the version in *A Noble Boke off Cookry* calls for almond milk.

24. Felets yne galentyne
This recipe is very similar to recipe 157 in *A Noble Boke off Cookry*.

To mak felettes in galentyne tak of the best of ribbes of pork and fley of the skyn and put the flesshe upon a broche and rost it till it be almost enoughe then tak it of and chope it in peces and put it in a pot with onyons butter and faire grece hole clowes maces quybibes and put it to gedur with a crust of bred and try it through a strener with whit wyne put ther to pouder of peper and put it in the pot and when it boilithe let it not be chargant and sesson it up with poudre of guingere and salt it and serue it. [A Noble Boke off Cookry (England, 1468)]

There are several versions of this recipe in other surviving cookbooks, such as the example below from *Two Fifteenth-Century Cookery-Books*, but only this version in *Wagstaff* and the one from *A Noble Boke off Cookry* specifically call for ribs of pork.

Fylettys en Galentyne. Take fayre porke, the fore quarter, an take of the skyne; an put the porke on a fayre spete, an rost it half y-now; than take it of, an smyte it in fayre pecys, and caste it on a fayre potte; than take oynonys, and schrede hem, an pele hem (an pyle hem nowt to smale), an frye in a panne of fayre grece; than caste hem in the potte to the porke; than take gode broth of moton or of beef, an caste ther-to, an than caste ther-to pouder pepyr, canel, clowys, an macys, an let hem boyle wyl to-gederys; than tak fayre brede, an vynegre, an stepe the brede with the same brothe, an strayne it on blode, with ale, or ellys sawnderys, and salt, an lat hym boyle y-now, an serue it forth.   [Two Fifteenth-Century Cookery-Books (England, 1430)]

25. Leche provene
This recipe is a very odd one. The combination of almond milk, eel, and onions is somewhat unusual in medieval English cookbooks, and the title doesn't make much sense and isn't similar to that of any other English recipe. However I did find the same recipe in the 14th century French source, *Enseignements qui enseingnent a apareillier toutes manieres de viandes*.

For milk of Provence - If you want to make milk of Provence, take almonds, then grind them and temper with wine and water, then take whole parsley and onions cut in rings and mix with eels, and fry all together; then take whole saffron and water and long pepper. [Enseignements (France, ca. 1300)]

The version in Enseignements highlights the issues in the *Wagstaff* version. The title is clearly mistranslated, turning "lait" (milk) into "leche" (slice), instead of being made with wine, the almond milk is tempered with "wine white wine", and the instruction to fry all the ingredients together was left out entirely.

26. Numbelys of purpas or of other fysche
Once again we have a clear parallel to a recipe in *A Noble Boke off Cookry* - in this case recipe number 158. Recipes for porpoise kidneys/entrails seem to be very uncommon as I could not find anything else that came close.

> To mak nombles of porpas or of other good fisshe and ye may cut som of the fisshe smalle and put it in the pot and draw a liour with cruste with the same blod and some of the brose and red wyne and put all to gedur in a pot and put thereto pouder of peper clowes and canelle and set it on the fyere and sesson it up with pouder guingere venygere and salt, and ye may mak nombles of congure codlinge or other good fisshe in the same manner and serue it. [A Noble Boke off Cookry (England, 1468)]

27. Purpayse yne Galanteyne
Porpoise is commonly mentioned in fish-day recipes, and "galantine" dishes are also very common, so it is surprising that there aren't any other recipes for porpoise galantine in surviving cookbooks. The closest recipe I could find is the following one from Le Viandier de Taillevent.

> Porpoise. Split it along the back, cook it in water, and slice it into strips like venison. Take some wine and water from your fish, grind ginger, cassia, cloves, grains of paradise, long pepper and a bit of saffron, [boil], and make a good clearish broth. It should not be too yellow. Serve it like a subtlety, with a White Dish. [Le Viandier de Taillevent (France, ca. 1380)]

The basic instructions are the same - slice the porpoise in strips, boil it in wine, and add spices - but the wording is different enough that it is not clear the recipes are related.

28. Purpayse or Venysone ine brothe

That this recipe starts off calling for "chickens of porpoise" suggests that there was a copying or translation error somewhere. There are no other recipes that use this phrase, nor are there any that include all of the words "porpoise", "venison", and "chicken". The closest I could find to this one are the following recipes for fish in gravy.

> Elys in Sorre. Take eles, and fle hem, and choppe hem in faire colpons, And wassh hem clene, and putte hem in a faire potte; and then take parcelly, oynons, and shrede togidre to the eles; And then take pouder of peper, and broth of fissh, and set hit ouer the fire, and lete hem boyle togidre; And then take a lofe of brede, and alay the brede in the the same broth, And drawe hit thorgh a streynour; And whan the eles ben almoost y-sodde ynowe, caste there-to; And lete hem boile togidre; and take hem vp fro the fire, and cast ther-to salte, vinegre, And serue hit forth. [Two Fifteenth-Century Cookery-Books (England, 1430)]

> Sore Sengle. Take Elys or Gurnard, and parte hem half in Wyne, and half in watere, in-to a potte; take Percely and Oynonys and hewe hem smalle; take Clowes or Maces and caste ther-on; take Safroun, and caste ther-to, and sette on the fyre, and let boyle tylle it be y-now; then sette it a-doun; take poudere Gyngere, Canelle, Galyngale, and temper it vppe with Wyne, and cast on the potte and serue forth. [Two Fifteenth-Century Cookery-Books (England, 1430)]

29. Hare yne cyve

"Civey" recipes usually involve meat and onions in a red-colored gravy. The meat is most commonly rabbit or hare, but can also be chicken.

There is a recipe in *A Noble Boke off Cookry* for hare in civey, but the wording and instructions are notably different.

> To make haires in covy boile a haire, rost hir and lard here then fry her in grece with pepper ale and onyons mynced small and colour it with saffron then lay the hair in a platter and pour on the covy and serue it. [A Noble Boke off Cookry (England, 1468)]

Interestingly, the same source has a recipe for rabbit in civey that is a slightly closer match.

> To mak conys in cevy smyt conys in small peces and sethe them in good brothe put ther to mynced onyons and grece and draw a liour of broun bred and blod and sesson it with venygar and cast on pouder and salt and serve it. [A Noble Boke off Cookry (England, 1468)]

While there are numerous other recipes for rabbit or hare in civey, none of them that I have found include the step of putting the boiled hare in cold water and picking them clean.

30. Hare yne papalde
This recipe appears to be a parallel of recipe 223 in *A Noble Boke off Cookry*.

> To mak haires in pardolous tak an haire and parboille hir in good brothe swong eggs ther to and hew fleshe smalle and cast it in the sewe and sethe them well then tak obleys or waiffurs and couche them in a platter and salt the sewe and put it upon the obleys and serue it. [A Noble Boke off Cookry (England, 1468)]

While the most of the pieces are there and seem to be in the same order, the *Wagstaff* version is missing the eggs and seems to be slightly more cryptic. Versions of this recipe from other sources more closely match the one in *Noble*, which suggests the omission of the eggs may have been a copying error.

Hares In Papdele. XXIIII. Take Hares parboile hem in gode broth. cole the broth and waisshe the fleyssh. cast azeyn to gydre. take obleys oþer wafrouns in stede of lozeyns. and cowche in dysshes. take powdour douce and lay on salt the broth and lay onoward an messe forth. [Forme of Cury (England, 1390)]

Harus in Perdoylyse. Take harys and perboyle hom, I rede, In goode brothe, kele hit for drede, And hew þy flesshe and cast þerinne. Take swongen eggus, no more ne myn, And cast in þy sewe and sethe hit þenne. Take obles and wafrons, as I þe kenne, Close hom in dysshes fare and wele. Salt þe sewe, so have þou cele, And lay hit above as gode men done, And messe hit forthe, Syr, at þo none. [Liber cure cocorum (England, 1430)]

31. Hare yne talbut

There are a few other recipes for "hares in talbotes" in surviving cookbooks, and the closest to the one above is from *Forme of Cury*. The seasoning is slightly different, and there are a couple of minor steps added, but otherwise it is essentially the same.

Hares In Talbotes. XXIII. Take Hares and hewe hem to gobettes and seeþ hem with þe blode unwaisshed in broth. and whan þey buth y nowh: cast hem in colde water. pyke and waisshe hem clene. cole the broth and drawe it thurgh a straynour. take oþer blode and cast in boylyng water seeþ it and drawe it thurgh a straynour. take Almaundes unblaunched. waisshe hem and grynde hem and temper it up with the self broth. cast al in a pot. tak oynouns and parboile hem smyte hem small and cast hem in to þis Pot. cast þerinne Powdour fort. vynegur an salt. [Forme of Cury (England, 1390)]

32. Conynggez in grave

While there are a handful of recipes for various meats in onion gravy, this particular combination of rabbit, spices, and almond milk appears to be unique. The closest recipe I could find that had all these ingredients is the following one from *Ancient Cookery*, however it adds several other items.

> Browet Browet of almayne. Take conynges and parboyle hom, and choppe hom on gobettus, and rybbes of porke or of kydde, and do hit in a pot, and sethe hit; then take almondes and grynde hom, and tempur hit up wyth broth of beef, and do hit in a pot; and take clowes, maces, pynes, ginger mynced, and raysynges of corance; and take onyons and boyle hom, then cut hom and do hom in the pot; and colour hit with saffron, and let hit boyle; and take the flesh oute from the brothe and caste therto; and take alkenet and frye hit, and do hit in the pot thurgh a streynour; and in the fettynge doun put therto a lytel vynegar, and pouder of gynger medelet togedur, and serve hit forth. [Ancient Cookery (England, 1425)]

If the almond milk is omitted then the recipe isn't too far off from recipe 133 in *A Noble Boke off Cookry*.

> To mak cony or malard in cevy tak cony henne or malard and rost them till they be almost enoughe or els chope them and fry them in freche grece and fry onyons mynced and put them in a pot and cast ther to freche brothe and half wyne clowes maces pouder of guinger and pepper and draw it with venygar and when it is boiled cast ther to thy licour and pouder of guingere and venygar and sesson it and serue it. [A Noble Boke off Cookry (England, 1468)]

33. Conynggez in Cyve

Rabbit in onion gravy was apparently a very popular dish, enough so that most medieval cookbooks have one or more version of the recipe. The version in *Wagstaff* includes aspects of several of them.

> Connynges In Cynee. XXV. Take Connynges and smyte hem on peces. and seeþ hem in gode broth, mynce Oynouns and seeþ hem in grece and in gode broth do þerto. drawe a lyre of brede. blode. vynegur and broth do þerto with powdour fort. [Forme of Cury (England, 1390)]

78

To mak conys in cevy smyt conys in small peces and sethe them in good brothe put ther to mynced onyons and grece and draw a liour of broun bred and blod and sesson it with venygar and cast on pouder and salt and serve it. [A Noble Boke off Cookry (England, 1468)]

Conynges in cyne. Take conynges and parboyle hom, and smyte hom on gobettes and sethe hom; and take onyons and mynce hom, and frye hom in grees, and do therto; and take bred steped in brothe and blode, and drawe up a lyoure (mixture) wyth brothe and vynegur, and do therin; and pouder of pepur and of clowes, and serve hit forthe. [Ancient Cookery (England, 1425)]

As with the above, the *Wagstaff* version calls for cut up chicken and onions, and is thickened using bread crumbs and blood. However the *Wagstaff* version also adds "good herbs", and uses wine in the thickening step instead of broth. In this way it is rather unusual.

34. Conyngges yne clere brothe

This recipe for "clear rabbit soup" is very similar to one by the same name in *Forme of Cury*.

Connynges In Clere Broth. XX.III. VI. Take Connynges and smyte hem in gobetes and waissh hem and do hem in feyre water and wyne, and seeþ hem and skym hem. and whan þey buth isode pyke hem clene, and drawe the broth thurgh a straynour and do the flessh þerwith in a Possynet and styne it. and do þerto vynegur and powdour or gynger and a grete quantite and salt after the last boillyng and serue it forth. [Forme of Cury (England, 1390)]

There are a couple of minor differences. *Wagstaff* uses broth instead of water, and omits the vinegar in favor of verjuice (both of which would add tartness), but otherwise the recipes are essentially the same.

35. Oysters in grave

While there are a number of other recipes with the same title in surviving cookbooks, the closest one is the following.

> Oystres in grauey. Take almondes, and blanche hem, and grinde hem, and drawe hem thorgh a streynour with wyne, and with goode fressh broth into gode mylke, and sette hit on the fire and lete boyle; and cast thereto Maces, clowes, Sugur, pouder of Ginger, and faire parboyled oynons myced; And then take faire oystres, and parboile hem togidre in faire water; And then caste hem there-to, And lete hem boyle togidre til they ben ynowe; and serue hem forth for gode potage. [Two Fifteenth-Century Cookery-Books (England, 1430)]

The use of almond milk instead of dairy suggests that this was intended as a recipe for fish days.

36. Oystres in Cyve

There are a handful of other recipes for "Oysters in Civey", but none of them are quite the same as this one. Some could be due to steps being omitted and replaced with the phrase "make heme up as thy dyde the conyngys al save the blode", but it's not completely clear which recipe is being referred to. Most likely they mean recipe 33 (Conynggez in Cyve) given above. With that for context, the following recipe from Forme of Cury seems to be the closest.

> OYSTERS IN CYNEE. XX.VI. III. Take Oysters parboile hem in her owne broth, make a lyour of crustes of brede & drawe it up wiþ the broth and vynegur mynce oynouns & do þerto with erbes. & cast the oysters þerinne. boile it. & do þerto powdour fort & salt. & messe it forth. [Forme of Cury (England, 1390)]

37. Chikens in gretney

While the title of the recipe most likely brings to mind the word "gratineé", it is much more likely to be a mispelling of "kirtin" as there are several contemporary recipes titled "chickens in kirtin", including one in *A Noble Boke off Cookry*.

To dight chekins in kirtyn tak iij pound of almondes made with good pik mylk with swet brothe and put it in a pot and put ther to clowes mace sugur and pynes hole and let it boile to gedur till it be honging and put ther to an unce of ginger and vinigar and put it in the pot then tak chekins ehalvyd / for a lord tak hole chekins and sethe them a litille then pull of the skyne and fry them in swete grece and put them in large dillies and pour on the ceripe and do ther on sugur and pouder of ginger and serue. [A Noble Boke off Cookry (England, 1468)]

38. Creteyney
There are a number of recipes with names similar to "cretonne", and in general they involve a broth made from milk thickened or colored with eggs. The version in Forme of Cury is shorter and less complicated than the one above, but still fits the stereotype.

> TXXIV - FOR TO MAKE CRAYTOUN. Tak checonys and schald hem and seth hem and grvnd gyngen' other pepyr and comyn and temper it up wyth god mylk and do the checonys theryn and boyle hem and serve yt forthe. [Forme of Cury (England, 1390)]

There is also a cretonne recipe in *Noble*, but it reads more like a recipe for fried chicken than a sort of soup. I suspect that it may be an error in which the start of a cretonne recipe was joined with the end of a recipe for funnel cakes.

> To mak cratonnes tak chekins and sethe them fley them and quarter them then grind pepper bred and comyne and boile the chekins in mylk then swinge eggs flour and hony togedure and put faire grece in a possuet and cast in the bater and stirr it till it be in many and serue it as friturs. [A Noble Boke off Cookry (England, 1468)]

39. Capons yne conceps
There is a recipe in *A Noble Boke off Cookry* that is clearly related to the one above, however it is much more abbreviated.

To mak capons in couns tak a capon and sethe it and hew it then grind pepper and bred and temper it with the capon then tak the whit of egg herd sodene and hew them small and boile the capons and colour it with saffron and lay yolks of eggs in the disshe hole and serue it. [A Noble Boke off Cookry (England, 1468)]

A recipe from Forme of Cury seems to be a much closer match, with much the same spicing and even including the instruction that the capon be half roasted.

Capouns In Councys. XXII. Take Capons and rost hem right hoot þat þey be not half y nouhz and hewe hem to gobettes and cast hem in a pot, do þerto clene broth, seeþ hem þat þey be tendre. take brede and þe self broth and drawe it up yferer, take strong Powdour and Safroun and Salt and cast þer to. take ayrenn and seeþ hem harde. take out the zolkes and hewe the whyte þerinne, take the Pot fro þe fyre and cast the whyte þerinne. messe the disshes þerwith and lay the zolkes hool and flour it with clowes. [Forme of Cury (England, 1390)]

40. Chikens yne caudelle

A caudle is sort of hot, thickened wine usually served as a beverage or soup. There is a recipe in *A Noble Boke off Cookry* that is very similar to the one above, though it doesn't include the instructions on how to arrange the chicken.

To mak chekins in cawdelle tak your chekins and boile them in good brothe and allay the brothe with yolks of eggs then tak poudur of guingere saffron and salt and set it on the fyere and serue it with the chekins in the disshe and the cawdell ther on. [A Noble Boke off Cookry (England, 1468)]

Other versions from Forme of Cury and Liber cure cocorum are almost identical to the one in *A Noble Boke off Cookry*, with the minor addition of stating that the chicken can be whole or sectioned.

Chykenns In Cawdel. XXXIII. Take Chikenns and boile hem in gode broth and ramme hem up. þenne take zolkes of ayrenn an þe broth and alye it togedre. do þerto powdour of gynger and sugur ynowh safroun and salt. and set it ouere the fyre withoute boyllyng. and serue the Chykenns hole oþer ybroke and lay þe sowe onoward. [Forme of Cury (England, 1390)]

Chekyns in Cawdel. In brothe þou boyle þy chekyns gode. Take 3olkes of eyren, Syr, for þo rode, Alye hom up with brothe forsayde. Take powder gyngur, abrayde, And sugur, and rew, and safron clere, And salt, and set hit over þo fyre. With owtyn boylyng messe hit forthe þenne. Þy chekyns hole take, I þe kenne, Of þay be brokyn, on dysshe hom lay, Helde hom þe sewe, as I þe say. [Liber cure cocorum (England, 1430)]

41. Soupes
This recipe is an oddity. If followed as written, the result would likely be honey-covered marrow on toast. Given that the other recipes for "sops", such as the ones given below, generally use almond milk as a base, I suspect that this recipe is a copying error.

To mak soupes dorrey tak almondes and bray them asid wring them up and boile them with wyn and temper them with wyne and salt then toost whit bred and lay it in a disshe and enbane it with wyne and pour it ouer the met and florisshe it with sugur and guingere and serue it. [A Noble Boke off Cookry (England, 1468)]

Sowpes Dorry. XX.IIII. II. Take Almaundes brayed, drawe hem up with wyne. ooile it, cast þeruppon safroun and salt, take brede itosted in wyne. lay þerof a leyne and anoþer of þe sewe and alle togydre. florish it with sugur powdour gyngur and serue it forth. [Forme of Cury (England, 1390)]

Soppes Dorre. Take rawe Almondes, And grynde hem in A morter, And temper hem with wyn and drawe hem thorgh a streynour; And lete hem boyle, And cast there-to Saffron, Sugur, and salt; And then take a paynmain, And kut him and tost him, And wete him in wyne, And ley hem in a dissh, and

83

caste the siryppe thereon, and make a dregge (Note: dredge. Douce MS. dragge) of pouder ginger, sugur, Canell, Clowes, and maces, And cast thereon; And whan hit is I-Dressed, serue it forth fore a good potage. [Two Fifteenth-Century Cookery-Books (England, 1430)]

42. Chaudone of Veel

This is another odd recipe, a sort of veal tripe with dumplings, and appears to be unique. The closest recipe I could find was from the 17th century A NEVV BOOKE of Cookerie.

To bake a Calues Chaldron. Parboyle it, and coole it, and picke out the Kernels, and cut it in small pieces: then season it with Pepper, Salt, and Nutmeg: put in a few sweet Hearbes chopt, a piece of sweet Butter, sprinckle it with Uergis, and so close it. When you serue it in, put to it a little of a Cawdle, made with Nutmeg, Uinegar, Butter, Sugar, and the yolkes of two newe layde Egges, a spoonefull of Sack, and the iuyce of an Orenge. [A NEVV BOOKE of Cookerie (England, 1615)]

There are other recipes for "chaudron", which is an archaic word for "entrails", usually calling for the offal of game birds but sometimes fish, and there's even a meatless version that uses nuts.

Chawdwyn. Take Gysers, lyuers, and hertes of Swannes, or of wilde gese; And if the guttes be fatte, slytte hem, and cast hem there-to, And boile hem in faire water; And then take hem vppe, And hew hem smale, and caste into the same broth ayene, but streyne hit thorgh a streynour firste; And caste thereto pouder of peper and of canell, and salt, and vinegre, And lete boile; And then take the blode of the swan, and fressh broth, and brede, and drawe hem thorgh a streynour and cast thereto, And lete al boyle togidre; And then take pouder of Gynger, whan hit is al-moost ynough, And caste there-to, And serue it forthe. [Two Fifteenth-Century Cookery-Books (England, 1430)]

Chaudewyne. Take the Guttes of fressh Samon, and do awey the gall; and slytte hem, and caste hem in a potte, and boyle hem in water right well; And ley hem vpon a borde, and hewe hem; And then stepe brede in the same licour, And cast som of the samon broth thereto, And drawe all thorgh a streynour; and then caste the hewen guttes and the drawen brede in a potte, and a litull wyn, pouder of Canell, or saffron, And lete boyle togidre; And cast there-to pouder of peper, Vinegre, and salt; And lete hit be rennyng.   [Two Fifteenth-Century Cookery-Books (England, 1430)]

To mak chawdwen de boyse tak noot kirnelles and fry them in oile then sethe them in almond mylk put ther to flour of ryse and other poudures and fry not kirnelles and colour them with saffron and serue them.   [A Noble Boke off Cookry (England, 1468)]

43. Chaudone of Pigges fete
This recipe is very clearly a match for recipe 159 from *A Noble Boke off Cookry.*

To mak chaudron of piggs feet take swines feet clene skalded and boile the [word illegible] and the eres in freche brothe then take them up and cutt them small and put them in a pot and the brothe and draw liour of whit bred and wyne and put them to gedur and mak foilis of past and cut iij small pilotes and frye them and sesson them up with pouder of pepper and salt and colour it to saffron and put the pilottes hote in disshes and put the sewe above and serue it.   [A Noble Boke off Cookry (England, 1468)]

The word "groyne" in *Wagstaff* (which is missing in *Noble*) most likely isn't a reference to genitals, but is probably a term borrowed from French. Cotgrave's 1611 French-English dictionary contains the following entry: "Groin de porceau. The snowt, or nose of a Hog." The combination of feet, ears and snout is somewhat common in medieval recipes because of the high gelatin content of each.

44. Bonse desire

In spite of the odd spelling in the title, this recipe is a variation of "Blanche Desyre", which is believed to be a corruption of the French "Blanc de Syrie" meaning "White of Syria". There are dozens of versions of this recipe, including two in *A Noble Boke off Cookry*.

> To mak bland sorre tak the mylk of almondes blanched mad with capon brothe then tak the braun of a capon and bet it in a mortair and mele the fishe and the mylk to gedur in the mortair with the pestelle and thik it with flour of rise and boile it put ther to sugur or hony and mak it stondinge then lesk it in dyshes and diaper it with turnsole and serue it. [A Noble Boke off Cookry (England, 1468)]

> To mak blank de fire tak ryse and wesshe it and grind it small and temper it up with almond mylk and boile it then tak the braun of capon or henne and hew it small and grind it with myed bred and sesson it with sugur and florishe it with almondes and serue it. [A Noble Boke off Cookry (England, 1468)]

45. Bruet of lumbardy

This recipe is almost identical to recipe 160 from *A Noble Boke off Cookry*, and is very similar to another in Forme of Cury.

> To mak Bruet of lombardye tak hennes conys or other flesshe soden tender and try it and put it in a pot do ther to mylk bred and yolks of eggs sodden hew and grind them and drawe them upe with juic of parsly put ther to grece or claryfied butter or the fat of pork and sesson it and salt and put ther to venygar and mak it lik blod with alkaned and serue it. [A Noble Boke off Cookry (England, 1468)]

> XXXII - FOR RO MAKE BRUET OF LOMBARDYE. Tak chekenys or hennys or othere flesch and mak the colowre als red as any blod and tak peper and kanel and gyngyner bred and grynd hem in a morter and a porcion of bred and mak that bruer thenne and do that flesch in that broth and mak hem

boyle togedere and stury it wel and tak eggys and temper hem wyth Jus of Parcyle and wryng hem thorwe a cloth and wan that bruet is boylyd do that therto and meng tham togedere wyth fayr grees so that yt be fat ynow and serve yt forthe. [Forme of Cury (England, 1390)]

The word "Lombardy" in the name is kind of an odd one. It appears in the name of a diverse array of medieval dishes, but there is no clear link between them. It may be that the recipes all came from the Lombardy region of Italy, or that the recipes were simply attributed to that region to make them sound more exotic.

46. Bruet of Almayne
There are similarly titled recipes in other sources, and while they all have some similarities none is a strong match for the one above.

XXXI - FOR TO MAKE BRUET OF ALMAYNE. Tak Partrichys rostyd and checonys and qualys rostyd and larkys ywol and demembre the other and mak a god cawdel and dresse the flesch in a dysch and strawe powder of galentyn therupon. styk upon clowys of gelofre and serve yt forthe. [Forme of Cury (England, 1390)]

Brewet Of Almony. XX.II. VII. Take Conynges or kiddes and hewe hem small on moscels oþer on pecys. parboile hem with the same broth, drawe an almaunde mylke and do the fleissh þerwith, cast þerto powdour galyngale & of gynger with flour of Rys. and colour it wiþ alkenet. boile it, salt it. & messe it forth with sugur and powdour douce. [Forme of Cury (England, 1390)]

Browet Browet of almayne. Take conynges and parboyle hom, and choppe hom on gobettus, and rybbes of porke or of kydde, and do hit in a pot, and fethe hit; then take almondes and grynde hom, and tempur hit up wyth broth of beef, and do hit in a pot; and take clowes, maces, pynes, ginger mynced, and rayfynges of corance ; and take onyons and boyle hom, then cut hom and do hom in the pot; and colour hit with saffron, and let hit boyle; and take the flesh oute from the brothe and caste therto; and take alkenet and frye hit, and do hit in the pot thurgh a streynour; and in the fettynge doun put therto a lytel vynegar, and pouder of gynger medelet togedur, and serve hit forth. [Ancient Cookery (England, 1425)]

Browet of almayne for x mees. Take iii lb. of almondes, and tempur hom, and drawe hom up with fresshe brothe of beef, and put into a pot; and take conynges parboyled, and choppe hom, and ribbes of porke chopped also; or elles take malardes chopped with the ribbes, and let hom fethe up with the mylke, and make the pottage rennynge; and take maces, clowes, pynes, ginger, mynced reyfynges of corance, sugre, and put therto; and take onyons mynced, and boyle hom in water, and after the first boyle dense hom out of the water, and cast hom into the pot, and let hom fethe up with the mylk, and colour hit with saffron; and take alkenet ii. penyworth, and frie hit in faire grese, and put the grese into a pot thurgh the streynour in the settynge doune; and take a lytel vynegur and pouder of ginger, and medel hit togedur, and cast therto, and dresse hit, and serve hit forthe. [Ancient Cookery (England, 1425)]

The word "Almayne" in the title of the recipe suggests that it is somehow related to Germany ("Allemagne" in French), but given how the related recipes all contain almonds it may be misnamed due to confusion of the two words or even intentional wordplay.

47. Bruet of Spayne

This recipe is a strong match for recipe 161 in *A Noble Boke off Cookry*. I have not found any other examples which include this combination of venison, wine, and almond milk.

To mak bruet of spayne take venyson and mak long lesshes then fry them in buttur and wesshe them in wyn then tak sugur almond mylk clowes maces quybibes and boile them to gedur and sesson them with poudure and venyger and serue it. [A Noble Boke off Cookry (England, 1468)]

48. Bruet roos

Here is another recipe that has a match with one in *A Noble Boke off Cookry* - this time number 162. This makes two recipes in a row and three out of the last four recipes, all of which appear in the same order (sometimes interspersed with other recipes) in both books.

> To mak bruet rose tak the flesshe of a Roo parboile it and try it and put it in a pot then tak the same brothe and other good brothe and draw it throughe a stren and put it in to the pot with onyons and erbes hole clowes maces and qubibes and set yt to the fyere and yf yt haue ned alay it with crustis of bred with a litille of the sam brothe and blod and colour it with saffron and salt it and cast ther to poudre of pepper and canelle and serue it. [A Noble Boke off Cookry (England, 1468)]

49. Chikens yne bruet

There doesn't appear to be any version of this recipe in other sources, which is a bit surprising given its simplicity. The closest match is probably the recipe below from *A Noble Boke off Cookry*.

> To dight chekyns in sauce tak chekine chapped for comons for a lord tak hole chekins and boile them with swet brothe of bef with a quantite of wyne and when they be ny enough tak out the chekins and bette the yolks of xl eggs in a mortair with saige and parsley and alay with good wyne and draw it throughe a stren put ther to poudre of clowes an unce of sugur an unce of canelles a litille veniger and colour it with saffron and salt then couche the chekins in dishes and put the ceryp in dyshes upon the mete and serue it. [A Noble Boke off Cookry (England, 1468)]

50. Stewe lumbarde

This recipe appears to be recipes 163 and 164 from *A Noble Boke off Cookry* run together.

To mak stewed lombard tak pork and rost it and chop it into a pot with wyne sugur and hole clowes onyons guingere saffron and sanders then fry almondes and temper them up with wyne pouder gyngyure canelle and galingale and serue it. [A Noble Boke off Cookry (England, 1468)]

To mak another stewed lombard take almondes and grind them and drawe them up with swet brothe of vele or of pork then tak the flesshe and pair it clene from the skyn hew it grind it and mele it with mynced dates raissins of corrans and good poudure and mak it in pilottes as gret as plomes and set the mylk on the fyer and stir it well when it boilithe cast in thy pilots and let them stewe upon the fyere and put ther to pouder and salt and serue it. [A Noble Boke off Cookry (England, 1468)]

The words that join these two, "coloure hit withe saffrone & saunders the chese" repeat the ingredients saffron and sandalwood, and add cheese, which doesn't appear anywhere in *Noble*. The most likely conclusion is that it is an error created when copying from one manuscript to another.

51. Stewy colops
A clear match of recipe 165 from *A Noble Boke off Cookry*. These two seem to be the only instances of such a simple recipe.

To mak stewed colopes tak collopes of venyson rostid and put them in a pot and do ther to hole clowes pouder of pepper canelle and other spice and boille it up with a gret part of swet brothe and sesson it up with pouder gyngir and the venyson and serue it. [A Noble Boke off Cookry (England, 1468)]

52. Bruet tuskyne
This recipe is similar to recipe 166 in *A Noble Boke off Cookry*, though the name in that source seems to have been changed somewhere along the way.

To mak Busbayne take mary and capons and other good flesshe and put it in a pot and chop chekins in peces and erbes hole clowes maces and pouder of pepper and sot them on the fyer and grind raw pork or vele with yolks of eggs and put ther to raissins of corane pouder and salt and saffron and mele them to gedure and when the potte boilethe put in the peletes like an hassille nott and cast them ther in boillinge and colour it with saffron put ther to parsly and other good erbes and boile it upe and put it to venyger and sesson it up with pouder and salt and serue it. [A Noble Boke off Cookry (England, 1468)]

There is another recipe for "tuskyn" in Liber cure cocorum, which is contemporary with the other two, though it leaves out the capon.

For Tuskyn. Take raw porke and hew hit smalle, And grynde in a morter; temper hit þou schalle With swongen egges, but not to þynne; In gryndynge, put powder of peper withinne, Þenne þis flessh take up in þy honde, And rolle hit on balles, I undurstonde, In gretnes of crabbes; I harde say In boylande water þou kast hom may. To harden þen take hom oute to cole, And play fresshe brothe fayre and wele; Þer in cast persoley, ysope, saveray, Þat smalle is hakked by any way. Alye hit with flour or brede for þy, Coloure hit with safroun for þe maystré; Cast powder of peper and clawes þer to, And take þy balles or þou more do, And put þer in; boyle alle in fere And serve hit forthe for tuskyne dere. [Liber cure cocorum (England, 1430)]

53. Bruet sarcenes
There are a couple of recipes for "Brewet of Saracen" in other sources, however neither of them include venison.

Bruette Sareson. Take Almaundys and draw a gode mylke and flowre of Rys, and Porke and Brawen of Capoun y-sode, or Hennys smale y-grounde, and boyle it y-fere, and do in-to the mylke; and than take pouder Gyngere, Sugre, and caste a-boue, an serue forth. [Two Fifteenth-Century Cookery-Books (England, 1430)]

FOR TO MAK A BRUET OF SARCYNESSE. Tak the lyre of the fresch Buf and bet it al in pecis and bred and fry yt in fresch gres tak it up and and drye it and do yt in a vessel wyth wyn and sugur and powdre of clowys boyle yt togedere tyl the flesch have drong the liycoure and take the almande mylk and quibibz macis and clowys and boyle hem togedere tak the flesch and do thereto and messe it forth. [Forme of Cury (England, 1390)]

Recipe 167 in *A Noble Boke off Cookry* also seems to be close, except that it calls for kid or veal in place of venison.

To mak a bruet of kiddes tak kide or vele and boile it chop it and dry it and put it into a pot then tak almonde mylk and drawe it with swet wyne and brothe do ther to hole clowes and flour of ryse alay it and aftur the boiling sesson it up with pouder of pepper gyngyr canelle and sugure and put it to venygar and salt and serue it. [A Noble Boke off Cookry (England, 1468)]

54. Bruet of kedes

This recipe is a clear match for recipe 167 in *A Noble Boke off Cookry*, with a couple of notable differences. In the *Wagstaff* version the kid is "tried" (separated) after boiling, but in *Noble* this is misread as "dry". In *Noble* (and in other similar recipes) flour of rice is used to thicken the broth, but in the *Wagstaff* version "rys" was miscopied as "rye".

To mak a bruet of kiddes tak kide or vele and boile it chop it and dry it and put it into a pot then tak almonde mylk and drawe it with swet wyne and brothe do ther to hole clowes and flour of ryse alay it and aftur the boiling sesson it up with pouder of pepper gyngyr canelle and sugure and put it to venygar and salt and serue it. [A Noble Boke off Cookry (England, 1468)]

There is a similar recipe in Forme of Cury, though it is the only version of "Bruet of Almaynne" that calls for kid.

Brewet Of Almony. XX.II. VII. Take Conynges or kiddes and hewe hem small on moscels oþer on pecys. parboile hem with the same broth, drawe an almaunde mylke and do the fleissh þerwith, cast þerto powdour galyngale & of gynger with flour of Rys. and colour it wiþ alkenet. boile it, salt it. & messe it forth with sugur and powdour douce. [Forme of Cury (England, 1390)]

55. Blaunche Bruet

This recipe is a match for recipe 168 in *A Noble Boke off Cookry*. Here, as in the recipe for "Bruet of kedes", the word "rys" was miscopied as "rye".

To mak blanche Bruet tak hennes and pork half rostid then chop them in peces and put them in a pot do ther to almond mylk and alay it up with flour of ryse or with whet floure and put ther to brothe or wyne hole clowes maces and sesson it with venygar pouder and sugur that is strawed with alkened and serue it. [A Noble Boke off Cookry (England, 1468)]

56. Sauce sarcenes

This recipe is a match for recipe 169 in *A Noble Boke off Cookry*.

To mak sauce sairsnet tak thik almond mylk and put it in a pott with flour of rise saffron maces guingere quybibes canelle and sugur and wet the botom of the disshes with swet brothe or withe wyne and put ther to hole maces and sesson it up with sugur venygar good pouder and guinger strawed with alkened and serve it. [A Noble Boke off Cookry (England, 1468)]

Saracen Sauce seems to have been popular as the recipe is included in several surviving cookbooks. Interestingly, the *Wagstaff* and *Noble* versions are the only ones from England that do not call for pomegranate.

Cxxxij - Sauke Sarsoun. Take Almaundys, and blaunche hem, and frye hem in oyle other in grece, than bray hem in a Mortere, and tempere hem with gode Almaunde mylke, and gode Wyne, and then the thrydde perty schal ben Sugre; and ȝif it be noȝt thikke y-nowe, a-lye it with Alkenade, and Florche (Note: Flourish; garnish) it a-bouyn with Pome-garned, and messe it; serue it forth. [Two Fifteenth-Century Cookery-Books (England, 1430)]

Sawse Sarzyne. XX.IIII. IIII. Take heppes and make hem clene. take Almaundes blaunched, frye hem in oile and bray hem in a morter with heppes. drawe it up with rede wyne, and do þerin sugur ynowhz with Powdour sort, lat it be stondyng, and alay it with flour of Rys. and colour it with alkenet and messe it forth. and florish it with Pommegarnet. If þou wilt in flesshe day. seeþ Capouns and take the brawnn and tese hem smal and do þerto. and make the lico of þis broth. [Forme of Cury (England, 1390)]

57. Veel in bucnade

There is a recipe in Forme of Cury with the same title, but its instructions are so at odds with those in *Wagstaff* that it almost seems to be a different recipe.

VEEL IN BUKNADE. C. XVIII. Take fayr Veel and kyt it in smale pecys and boile it tendre in fyne broth oþer in water. þanne take white brede oþer wastel, and drawe þerof a white ... lyour wiþ fyne broth, and do þe lyour to the Veel, & do safroun þerto, þanne take parsel & bray it in a morter & the Juys þerof do þerto, and þanne is þis half zelow & half grene. þanne take a porcioun of wyne & powdour marchant & do þerto and lat it boile wele, and do þerto a litel of vynegur. & serue forth. [Forme of Cury (England, 1390)]

Bukkenade recipes are very common in medieval cookbooks, so it's not surprising that *A Noble Boke off Cookry* has one (recipe 2). However, that recipe does not match the *Wagstaff* version either.

To mak buknad tak vele smale and vele parboiled then gader up the flesh and fireyn the broth through a stren and put it in to the pot and sett it on the fyer and put ther to onyons mynced pouder of pepper powder of cloves and canelle and in the boiling put in the fleshe then tak raw yolkes in a bolle and cast ther to the het brothe and mele it well to gedere and in the setting downe put in the egg and stirr it to geder in the setting down and geve it a litill color of saffron and salt it and serue it. [A Noble Boke off Cookry (England, 1468)]

58. Pynonade

This recipe is not like any other in medieval cookbooks. It might be a cross between another pineade recipe and one for quinade (made from quince), but there's no clear evidence to prove such. The closest of the pinade recipes is probably the following one from Forme of Cury.

Pynnonade. XX.II. XI. Take Almandes iblaunched and drawe hem sumdell thicke with gode broth oþer with water and set on the fire and seeþ it, cast þerto zolkes of ayrenn ydrawe. take Pynes yfryed in oyle oþer in grece and þerto white Powdour douce, sugur and salt. & colour it wiþ alkenet a lytel. [Forme of Cury (England, 1390)]

As an illustration of how different pineade recipes can be, here are two others.

XXXII - For To Make A Pynade Or Pyvade. Take Hony and Rotys of Radich and grynd yt smal in a morter and do yt thereto that hony a quantite of broun sugur and do thereto. Tak Powder of Peper and Safroun and Almandys and do al togedere boyl hem long and hold yt in a wet bord and let yt kele and messe yt and do yt forth. [Forme of Cury (England, 1390)]

iij - Pynade. Take Hony and gode pouder Gyngere, and Galyngale, and Canelle, Pouder pepir, and graynys of parys, and boyle y-fere; than take kyrnelys of Pynotys and caste ther-to; and take chyconys y-sothe, and hew hem in grece, and caste ther-to, and lat sethe y-fere; and then lat droppe ther-of on a knyf; and ȝif it cleuyth and wexyth hard, it ys y-now; and then putte it on a chargere tyl it be cold, and mace (Note: A. make) lechys, and serue with other metys; and ȝif thou wolt make it in spycery, then putte non chykonys ther-to. [Two Fifteenth-Century Cookery-Books (England, 1430)]

The first one, which calls for radishes, is an oddity in that it doesn't call for pine nuts. The second one is the infamous "chicken brittle" recipe, which I believe to be one of the worst copy errors ever.

59. Kyd stewyde
This short and simple recipe is another one with a clear match in *A Noble Boke off Cookry*, this time recipe number 170.

> To stewe a kid tak a kid and rost yt a litille and chop it in peces raw and put it in the pot do ther to erbes onyons and swet brothe and wyne hole clowes maces and pouder and sethe them and sesson them up with guinger galingale and a litille lier of bred saffron and salt and serve it. [A Noble Boke off Cookry (England, 1468)]

60. Stewyde pertryche
This recipe is a match for number 171 from *A Noble Boke off Cookry*. The only real differences are that the *Wagstaff* version omits the cloves and substitutes verjuice for vinegar.

> To stewe a pertuche or a wod cok and draw them and wesshe them clene and chope them with hole clowes and peper and couche them in an erthen pot put ther to dates mynced gret raisins of corans wyne and swet brothe salt it and cover the pot and set it on the fyer when it is enoughe sesson it with pouder of guinger and venygar and colour it with saffron and serue it. [A Noble Boke off Cookry (England, 1468)]

61. A losede beef
In spite of the different wording, this recipe is a match for number 172 from *A Noble Boke off Cookry*. In this case the *Wagstaff* version omits pepper and replaces galingale (a spice) with galantine (a sauce

or type of dish). Given the context of "... aley hit up withe sause gynger or galantyne ..." this change still makes sense.

> To mak a lowsid bef tak leney beef and cut it in thyn lesks and lay them abrod then tak the fat of moton or of beef erbes or onyons chopped small put ther to pouder of pepper and salt then tak the sewet and the erbes and lay upon the leskes and rolle them to gedur and put them on a broche and rost them welle and endor them or els ye may put them in a pot and put ther to good brothe and wyne then tak clowes maces onyons and erbes and chope them smale and put ther to pouder of pepper and saffron then salt it and alay it up with guinger and galingalle and stewe it up and serue it. [A Noble Boke off Cookry (England, 1468)]

To further confuse things, a version from *Two Fifteenth-Century Cookery-Books* differs from the other two by seasoning dish, not with a sauce, but with ginger and cinnamon.

> xxx - Alows de Beef or de Motoun. Take fayre Bef of the quyschons, (Note: Cushions) and motoun of the bottes, and kytte in the maner of Stekys; than take raw Percely, and Oynonys smal y-scredde, and ʒolkys of Eyroun sothe hard, and Marow or swette, and hew alle thes to-geder smal; than caste ther-on poudere of Gyngere and Saffroun, and tolle hem to-gederys with thin hond, and lay hem on the Stekys al a-brode, and caste Salt ther-to; then rolle to-gederys, and putte hem on a round spete, and roste hem til they ben y-now; than lay hem in a dysshe, and pore ther-on Vynegre and a lityl verious, and pouder Pepir ther-on y-now, and Gyngere, and Canelle, and a fewe ʒolkys of hard Eyroun y-kremyd ther-on; and serue forth. [Two Fifteenth-Century Cookery-Books (England, 1430)]

62. Pyke in sauce
This recipe is a close match for number 173 in *A Noble Boke off Cookry*.

> To dight a pik in sauce tak and dight the pouche and the fee of a pik and sethe it half in wyne and half in water cast ther to

parsly and onyons mynced smale boile them well and sethe pik
in good brothe and as it boilithe tak of the grece and cast yt to
the pouche and fee then tak som payn mayn cutt thyn as
brewes and toist it on a gredirne then mynce the pouche and
the fee and alay it up with ale and cast ther to venygar then lay
the pik in a chargiour and the resset with the pouche and the
fee aboue and serue it furthe. [A Noble Boke off Cookry
(England, 1468)]

There is a version of the same recipe in *Two Fifteenth-Century
Cookery-Books* which clarifies the word "fee" to mean "liver".

Pike boyled. Take and make sauce of faire water, salt, and a
litull Ale and parcelly; and then take a pike, and nape him, and
drawe him in the bely, And slytte him thorgh the bely, bak, and
hede and taile, with a knyfe in to peces; and smyte the sides in
quarters, and wassh hem clene; And if thou wilt have him
rownde, schoche him by the hede in the backe, And drawe him
there, And skoche him in two or iij. peces in the bak, but noȝt
thorgh; And slyt the pouuche, And kepe the fey or the lyuer,
and kutte awey the gall. And whan the sauce biginneth to
boyle, skem hit, And wassh the pike, and cast him there-in,
And caste the pouche and fey there-to, And lete hem boyle
togidre; And then make the sauce thus: myce the pouche and
fey, in a litul gravey of the pike, And cast there-to pouder of
ginger, vergeous, mustarde, and salt, And serue him forth hote.
[Two Fifteenth-Century Cookery-Books (England, 1430)]

63. Turbut rostyde in sauce

This recipe is a close match for number 174 in *A Noble Boke off
Cookry*.

To dight turbot rost in sauce tak and cutt away the fyn of the
turbotte and cutt the fisshe in the manner of felettes and put
them on a round broche and when it rostis springle on salt
then tak vergius venyger or wyn and pouder of guinger and
canelle and cast ther to in the rosting and set a vesselle under
to kep that fallithe and cast it on agayne and when it is rost cast

the sauce upon the fisshe in disshes and serue it. [A Noble Boke off Cookry (England, 1468)]

As with the recipe for pike above, there is also a version of this recipe in *Two Fifteenth-Century Cookery-Books*. Curiously, It retains the word hastlet/hastling which *Noble* replaces with fillet.

> Turbut roste ensauce. Take a Turbut, and kut of the vynnes in maner of a hastelette, and broche him on a rounde broche, and roste him; And whan hit is half y-rosted, cast thereon smale salt as he rosteth. And take also as he rosteth, vergeous, or vinegre, wyne, pouder of Gynger, and a litull canell, and cast thereon as he rosteth, And holde a dissh vnderneth, fore spilling of the licour; And whan hit is rosted ynowe, hete the same sauce ouer the fire, And caste hit in a dissh to the fissh all hote, And serue it forth. [Two Fifteenth-Century Cookery-Books (England, 1430)]

64. Salmone rostyde in sauce

This recipe is a close match to recipe 175 in *A Noble Boke off Cookry*. The only significant differance is that the *Noble* version does not allow for the use of vinegar in the sauce.

> To mak samon rost in sauce tak a samon and cutt hym in round peces and rost hym on a gredirne and tak wyn and pouder of canelle and draw them throughe a stren and mynce onyans smalle and do ther to and boile them then tak vergius pouder of peper and guinger and salt and do ther to then lay the samon in a disshe and pour on the ceripe and serue it. [A Noble Boke off Cookry (England, 1468)]

The same recipe (with the vinegar option) in other cookbooks as well, suggesting a certain amount of popularity.

> Samon roste in Sauce. Take a Salmond, and cut him rounde, chyne and all, and roste the peces on a gredire; And take wyne, and pouder of Canell, and drawe it thorgh a streynour; And take smale myced oynons, and caste there-to, and lete hem boyle; And then take vynegre, or vergeous, and pouder ginger,

and cast there-to; And then ley the samon in a dissh, and cast the sirip theron al hote, and serue it forth. [Two Fifteenth-Century Cookery-Books (England, 1430)]

Samon rostyd in sause. Cutte thy samon in Rownde pecys and roste hit on a roste Yre take wyne and powder of cannell and draw hem throwgh a streynner. Do ther to onyons mynsed small boyle hit well take vynegyr or verius and pouder of gynger and salt do ther to lay the samon In dyshys and pore the syrrppe ther on and serue forth. [MS Pepys 1047 (England, ca. 1500)]

65. Brawne in confyte

This recipe is a close match to recipe 176 from *A Noble Boke off Cookry*, with the odd exception that instead of "brawn" (meat) the *Noble* version calls for "bream" (a type of fish).

To dight breme in comfet tak and sethe a freche breme tille he be enoughe then grind it in a mortair and temper it with almond mylk and drawe it throwe a stren in to a pott put ther to suger pouder of pepper canelle clowes and guingere and boile it then tak it out of the pot and put it into alynclothe and pres out the thyn then tak the ribbes of a bore and couch them along through the leske and serue one or ij in a disshe. [A Noble Boke off Cookry (England, 1468)]

There are two versions of this recipe in *Two Fifteenth-Century Cookery-Books* that also call for brawn, which leads me to think that the fish version is in error.

Brawn in comfyte. Take Freyssch Brawn and sethe yt y-now, and pare it and grynde it in a mortere, and temper it with Almand mylke, and draw it thorw a straynoure in-to a potte, and caste ther-to Sugre y-now, and powder of Clowys, and let boyle; then take floure of Canelle, and pouder of Gyngere; and then take it out of the potte, an putte it in a lynen clothe and presse it, but lat it boyle so longe in the potte tylle it be alle thikke; than take it vppe and presse it on a clothe, and then leche it fayre with a knyff, but not to thinne; and than ʒif thou wolt, thou my3ht take the Rybbys of the bore al bare, and chete hem enlongys thorw the lechys, an so serue forth a leche or to in euery dysshe. [Two Fifteenth-Century Cookery-Books (England, 1430)]

Brawne in confite. Take fressh brawne, and seth it ynowe; pare hit, and grinde hit in a morter, and temper it with almond mylke, and draw it thorgh a Streynour into a potte, and cast thereto Sugour ynowe, and pouder of Clowes, and lete boyle; and take ffloure of Canell, or powder, a goode quantite, and caste there-to. And lete boyle, and caste there-to powder of ginger; And then take it vp oute of the potte, And put in a lynnen clothe and presse it; lete hem boile so long in the potte that it be thik, And then take hit vppe, and presse it in the clothe; And then leche hit faire, but not to thyn; And then take the ribbes of the boor, and al bare, and set hem enlonge the leches, And serue it forthe .ij. or iij. leches in a dissh. [Two Fifteenth-Century Cookery-Books (England, 1430)]

66. Leche Lumbarde

There is a similarly titled recipe in *A Noble Boke off Cookry*, recipe 22, but it appears to be incomplete. This could have been a copy or transcription error, or one introduced when Robina Napier transcribed the text back in 1882. The fact that the rest of the recipe doesn't at all resemble the *Wagstaff* version leads me to think they're not the same recipe.

Boile gadur of the skome and set it to the fyere agayne put ther to pouder of pepper canelle and grated bred and stirre it well to gedur colour it withe saffron and sanders and in the settinge doun do ther to a litill venygar mellid with pouder of guinger and stirr it and let it be stif then gadur it up in a clothe and splat it some dele abrod and couer it with the same clothe till it be colde and lay ij or iij lesks in a dyshe and straw ther on pouder of guinger mellid with sugur and serue it. [A Noble Boke off Cookry (England, 1468)]

Most of the other recipes for Leche Lumbard start with instructions for preparing raw meat - usually pork. There is one version from *Two Fifteenth-Century Cookery-Books* though that starts with dates.

> Leche lumbarde. Take Dates, and do awey the stones; and seth hem in swete wyne; and take hem vppe, and grinde hem in a morter, and drawe hem thorgh a streynour with a litull swete wyne and sugur; and caste hem in a potte, and lete boyle til it be stiff; and then take hem vppe, and ley hem vp apon a borde; and then take pouder ginger, Canell, and wyn, and melle al togidre in thi honde, and make it so stiff that hit woll be leched; And if hit be not stiff ynowe, take hard yolkes of eyren and creme thereon, or elles grated brede, and make it thik ynogh; take Clarey, and caste thereto in maner of sirippe, whan thou shall serue hit forthe. [Two Fifteenth-Century Cookery-Books (England, 1430)]

67. Tayle

There are a number of recipes in medieval cookbooks for "Tayles", or almond-milk jelly slices, but nothing that quite matches in *A Noble Boke off Cookry*. One of the closest to the *Wagstaff* version is the following recipe from *Two Fifteenth-Century Cookery-Books*

> xlviij - Tayloures. Take a gode mylke of Almaundys y-draw with Wyne an Water, an caste hym in-to a potte, and caste gret Roysouns of corauns, Also mencyd Datys, Clowes, Maces, Pouder Pepir, Canel, Safroun, and a gode dele Salt, and let boyle a whyle; than take it and ly it wyth Flowre of Rys, or ellys with Brede y-gratyd, and caste ther-to Sugre, and serue forth lyke Mortrewys, and caste pouder of Gyngere a-boue y-now. [Two Fifteenth-Century Cookery-Books (England, 1430)]

68. Blaunche de sorre

"Blanc de Syrie" is one of the more popular dishes in medieval cookbooks. It is usually a dish of capon meat in a sauce of almond milk or rice, thickened to the point that it can be sliced. There are two versions of this recipe in *A Noble Boke off Cookry*, but neither one seems to be the source for the recipe above.

To mak bland sorre tak the mylk of almondes blanched mad with capon brothe then tak the braun of a capon and bet it in a mortair and mele the fishe and the mylk to gedur in the mortair with the pestelle and thik it with flour of rise and boile it put ther to sugur or hony and mak it stondinge then lesk it in dyshes and diaper it with turnsole and serue it. [A Noble Boke off Cookry (England, 1468)]

To mak blank de fire tak ryse and wesshe it and grind it small and temper it up with almond mylk and boile it then tak the braun of capon or henne and hew it small and grind it with myed bred and sesson it with sugur and florishe it with almondes and serue it. [A Noble Boke off Cookry (England, 1468)]

The closest match appears to be the following recipe from *Two Fifteenth-Century Cookery-Books*. It has a bit more detail, which makes it easier to understand the instructions in the *Wagstaff* version.

xxj - Blandissorye. Take almaundys, an blawnche hem, an grynde hem in a morter, an tempere hem with freysshe brothe of capoun or of beef, an swete wyne; an ʒif it be lente or fyssday, take brothe of the freysshe fysshe, an swete wyne, an boyle hem to-gederys a goode whyle; thenne take it up, an caste it on a fayre lynen clothe that is clene an drye, an draw under the clothe, wyth a ladel, alle the water that thow may fynde, ryth as thow makyst cold creme; thanne take owt of the potte, an caste it in-to a fayre potte, an let it boyle; an thanne take brawn of Capoun, an tese it smal an bray it ina morter: or ellys on a fyssday take Pyke or Elys, Codlyng or Haddok, an temper it with almaun mylke, an caste Sugre y-now ther-to; An than caste hem in-to the potte and lete hem boyle to-gederys a goode whyle: thenne take it owt of the potte alle hote, an dresse it in a dysshe, as meni don cold creme, an sette ther-on Red Anys in comfyte, or ellys Allemaundys blaunchid, an thanne serue it forth for a goode potage. [Two Fifteenth-Century Cookery-Books (England, 1430)]

69. Blaw maungere

"Blancmanger" is by far the most common recipe appearing in medieval cookbooks. There are two versions in *A Noble Boke off Cookry*, but only one is a meat-day recipe and both of them merged don't quite match the *Wagstaff* version.

> To mak blanche mange of flesshe tak ryse and wesshe it and draw it throughe a stren and temper it with almond mylk then teese the braun of capon or henn small and put the rise to the mylke and boile it and charge it with the tosed flesshe sesson it with sugur and florisshe it with almonds and serue it. [A Noble Boke off Cookry (England, 1468)]

> To mak blank mang of fisshe tak a pound of rise and sethe it and bray it till it brests and cast it to almond mylk then tak a tenche or a lampry and cast ther to and sethe them to gedure and serwe it. [A Noble Boke off Cookry (England, 1468)]

Even if the fish-day instructions are left out of both the *Noble* and *Wagstaff* recipes, they still don't quite match up. Nor does the *Wagstaff* version match any of the other blancmanger recipes I've found.

70. Blaunche Doucet

This recipe is odd in that, while it seems similar to a large number of recipes in other sources, doesn't seem to closely match any of them. The ingredients are similar to those in "Blanch Mortrews" or "Blanc Desire", both of which appear in *A Noble Boke off Cookry*, but there are aspects of the recipe that don't appear in either. The use of egg yolks as a garnish (replaced with dough in the fish-day version) is particularly unusual.

> To mak blanched mortrus tak and sethe hennes and freche pork to gedur then bray unblanched almondes and temper them with clene brothe and alay the fleshe small ground ther to put ther to flour of rise and do all to gedur and cast in pouder of guingere and sugur and luk it be not thyn salt it and serue it. [A Noble Boke off Cookry (England, 1468)]

To mak blank de fire tak ryse and wesshe it and grind it small
and temper it up with almond mylk and boile it then tak the
braun of capon or henne and hew it small and grind it with
myed bred and sesson it with sugur and florishe it with
almondes and serue it. [A Noble Boke off Cookry
(England, 1468)]

It may be that this is a bastardized version of one of these or some
other recipe, or that it was meant exactly as presented.

71. Chikeney
This is one of a very small number of medieval recipes that call for
acorns, and the only one I have found that uses them to make a
sort of sauce or soup. Despite the title, the recipe doesn't actually
include any chicken. It is possible that the last instruction, "& set a
bovyne", is a suggestion to serve over roasted poultry.

72. Blanke desire
While there is a recipe for "Blanc Desire" in *A Noble Boke off
Cookry*, that one has different ingredients (e.g. poultry instead of
pork) and doesn't really seem to be the same dish.

To mak blank de fire tak ryse and wesshe it and grind it small
and temper it up with almond mylk and boile it then tak the
braun of capon or henne and hew it small and grind it with
myed bred and sesson it with sugur and florishe it with
almondes and serue it. [A Noble Boke off Cookry (England,
1468)]

There's a recipe in Forme of Cury that is much closer, but even it
has some significant differences.

XIX - FOR TO MAKE BLANK DE SUR. Tak the zolkys of
Eggs sodyn and temper it wyth mylk of a kow and do ther'to
Comyn and Safroun and flowr' of ris or wastel bred mycd and
grynd in a morter and temper it up wyth the milk and mak it
boyle and do ther'to wit of Egg' corvyn smale and tak fat chese

and kerf ther'to wan the licour is boylyd and serve it forth.
[Forme of Cury (England, 1390)]

73. Dage

The title of this recipe looks like it might be a copy error for
"Sage", but if so then there must be other errors because the recipe
does not match any of the surviving recipes for pork in sage sauce.
Nor could I find any other recipes that were similar, so this one
may be unique.

74. Sypers

The title of this recipe suggests that it is a version of "Viand
Cypress", but none of the other recipes are more than superficially
like this one. The closest are the two below, neither of which call
for figs and currants.

> To mak viand de cipre, tak the braun of capon or of henne
> parboille it and dry it then hew it smalle in a mortair and putt
> ther to almond mylk and lay it up with amydon or with flour of
> rise coloure it with saffron and boille it and chargant it with the
> braed braun and sesson it with sugur and florishe it with
> almondes and serue it.   [A Noble Boke off Cookry
> (England, 1468)]

> lxlv. Vyaunde cypre. Take mele & pyke out the stones &
> grynde hem smale, & drawe hem throw a straynour, take mede
> other wyne y funfryt in suger & do these therin, do therto
> poudour & salt & lay hit with flour of rys, & loke that hit be
> stondyng, if thou wolt on flesche day: take hennes and pork y
> sode and grynde smale & do therto & messe hit forth.
> [Fourme of Curye (England, 1390)]

75. Floreye

There are several similar recipes in surviving medieval cookbooks,
but none are an exact match for this one. Two of the closest ones
are in *A Noble Boke off Cookry* and Forme of Cury.

To mak rose, tak flour of ryse and temper it with almond mylk and mak it chaungynge then tak the braun of capon or of henne sodyn and grind it and charge it ther with and colour it with sanders and blod and fors it with clowes and maces and sesson it with sugur and serue it. [A Noble Boke off Cookry (England, 1468)]

XLI - For to make Rosee. Tak the flowris of Rosys and wasch hem wel in water and after bray hem wel in a morter and than tak Almondys and temper hem and seth hem and after tak flesch of capons or of hennys and hac yt smale and than bray hem wel in a morter and than do yt in the Rose so that the flesch acorde wyth the mylk and so that the mete be charchaunt and after do yt to the fyre to boyle and do thereto sugur and safroun that yt be wel ycolowrd and rosy of levys and of the forseyde flowrys and serve yt forth. [Forme of Cury (England, 1390)]

The one from *A Noble Boke off Cookry* is interesting because of the change from "flowers of rose" to "flour of rice". Given that almond milk thickens when cooked - though not as much as almond milk and rice flour - it is difficult to determine which one is the definitive version.

76. Creme boyled
There are several version of this thickened-cream recipe, including the one below from *A Noble Boke off Cookry*, but none are an exact match for the *Wagstaff* recipe.

To mak creme buile tak cow creme and yolks of eggs drawe and well bet that it be stonding and put ther to sugur and colour it with saffron and salt it then lesk it in dyshes and plant ther in floures of borage and serue it. [A Noble Boke off Cookry (England, 1468)]

77. Lyed mylke
While there are dozens of similar medieval recipes for "alayed

milk" or "larded milk", this recipe is a clear match for recipe 179 from *A Noble Boke off Cookry*.

> To mak alayd mylk take cow mylk and sugur and put it in a pot and set it on the fyere and when it boilithe alay it up with yolks of eggs and let it be rynynge and not chargant then tak whit bred and cut it in thyn peces and lay them in a disshe and let the mylk be somewhat salt and serue it furthe. [A Noble Boke off Cookry (England, 1468)]

78. Moretruys of wresch fysch

This recipe is similar to recipe 25 from *A Noble Boke off Cookry*.

> To mak mortins of fyshe tak codlinge haddok whiting or thornbak and sethe it and pik out the bones and pull of the skyne then bet the fishe in a mortair with the lever of the same fysche and temper it up with almond mylk or cow creme and put it in a clene pot and let it boile and put ther to sugur and hony and alay thy potage with fleur of rise draw with milk through a strein and stirr it well and mak it stondinge then drese v or vi lesks in a dyshe and cast on pouder guingyur mellid with sugur and serue it. [A Noble Boke off Cookry (England, 1468)]

That being said, there is a recipe in MS Pepys 1047 that is closer in wording.

> To make mortrose of Fyshe. Take hownde fyshe haddock or codlyng seth hit and pyke hit clene fro the bonys take a way the skyn and grynde the lyver ther with blanched almounds And temper thy mylke with the broth of the fresh Fyshe and make a gode mylke of do ther to myad of white brede and sugure set hit to the fyre when hit boylys loke hit be stondyng mese serue hit furth strow on Blawnche powdyr. [MS Pepys 1047 (England, ca. 1500)]

The inclusion of the words "fresh Fyshe" in MS Pepys 1047 suggests that "wresch" in the title of the *Wagstaff* version is a copying error.

79. Mortruys of flesch

This recipe is similar to the "blanched mortrus" recipe in *A Noble Boke off Cookry*, but that one is thickened with rice flour rather than the eggs.

> To mak blanched mortrus tak and sethe hennes and freche pork to gedur then bray unblanched almondes and temper them with clene brothe and alay the fleshe small ground ther to put ther to flour of rise and do all to gedur and cast in pouder of guingere and sugur and luk it be not thyn salt it and serue it. [A Noble Boke off Cookry (England, 1468)]

There are several other recipes for mortrews, but none are a close match. Interestingly, all of them also call for rice flour, which leads me to wonder if that ingredient was accidentally left out of the *Wagstaff* version.

> Cxx - Whyte Mortrewys of Porke. Take lene Porke, and boyle it; blaunche Almandys, and grynd hem, and temper vppe with the brothe of the porke, and lye hem vppe with the Flowre of Rys, an lete boyle to-gederys, but loke that the porke be smal grounde y-now; caste ther-to Myncyd Almaundys y-fryid in freysshe grece; then sesyn hem vppe alle flatte in a dysshe; throw ther-to Sugre y-now and Salt; and atte the dressoure, strawe ther-on pouder Gyngere y-mellyd with Almaundys. [Two Fifteenth-Century Cookery-Books (England, 1430)]

> lxix - Whyte Mortrewes. Take Almaunde Mylke and Floure of Rys, and boyle it y-fere; thenne take Capoun and Hennys, and sethe hem and bray hem as smal as thou may, and ly (Note: Allay; mix) it with an Ey (Note: Egg) or to, and also a-lye it vppe with the mylke of Almaundys, and make hem chargeaunt as Mortrewes schuld be, and dresse hem forth, and caste Canel a-boue, or Gyngere. Blanke pouder is best. [Two Fifteenth-Century Cookery-Books (England, 1430)]

> Mortrews Blank. XX.II. VI. Take Pork and Hennes and seeþ hem as to fore. bray almandes blaunched, and temper hem up with the self broth. and alye the fleissh with the mylke and white flour of Rys. and boile it. & do þerin powdour of gyngur

sugar and look þat it be stondyng. [Forme of Cury (England, 1390)]

80. Blaunch mortruys of fisch
As with *Wagstaff* recipe 78 (Moretruys of wresch fysch), this recipe is also similar to recipe 25 in *A Noble Boke off Cookry*, though it calls for rice flour that the *Wagstaff* omits.

> To mak mortins of fyshe tak codlinge haddok whiting or thornbak and sethe it and pik out the bones and pull of the skyne then bet the fishe in a mortair with the lever of the same fysche and temper it up with almond mylk or cow creme and put it in a clene pot and let it boile and put ther to sugur and hony and alay thy potage with fleur of rise draw with milk through a strein and stirr it well and mak it stondinge then drese v or vi lesks in a dyshe and cast on pouder guingyur mellid with sugur and serue it. [A Noble Boke off Cookry (England, 1468)]

There are several other recipes similarly titled, in the contemporary cookbooks, but none are close matches.

81. Blaunch mortruys
While there are other recipes for "blanc mortrews", all of the others call for pork rather than capons or game birds. Therefore this recipe appears to be unique.

82. Paynd foundow
This recipe is clearly a version of the following recipe from Forme of Cury.

> Payn Fondew. XX.II. XIX. Take brede and frye it in grece oþer in oyle, take it and lay it in rede wyne. grynde it with raisouns take hony and do it in a pot and cast þerinne gleyres of ayrenn wiþ a litel water and bete it wele togider with a sklyse. set it ouer the fires and boile it. and whan the hatte arisith to goon ouer, take it adoun and kele it, and whan it is

110

þer clarified; do it to the oþere with sugur and spices. salt it and loke it be stondyng, florish it with white coliaundre in confyt. [Forme of Cury (England, 1390)]

What is interesting is that despite the differences in directions and ingredients, both recipes include the step of clarifying the mixture (the egg whites bind to the impurities during boiling and then are skimmed off) and both state that the final dish should be "stondyng."

83. Caudell

There are a large number of caudle recipes in other cookbooks, but none are worded quite like the above. In terms of ingredients, the *Wagstaff* recipe is reasonably close to the this simple caudle found in *Two Fifteenth-Century Cookery-Books*.

> Caudell. Take faire tryed yolkes of eyren, and cast in a potte; and take good ale, or elles good wyn, a quantite, and sette it ouer the fire/ And whan hit is at boyling, take it fro the fire, and caste there-to saffron, salt, Sugur; and ceson hit vppe, and serue hit forth hote. [Two Fifteenth-Century Cookery-Books (England, 1430)]

84. Caudell fery

As with the recipe for caudle, there are many recipes for "caudle ferry" in the surviving medieval cookbooks. In this case there are three with that title in *A Noble Boke off Cookry*, but none is quite the same as the *Wagstaff* version.

> To mak cawdelle ferry tak unblanched almonds wesshe them and grind them and temper them up with wyne and drawe it throughe a canvas into a pot and colour it with saffron and alay it up with amydon or flour of rise and se that it be thik sesson it with sugur and florishe it with maces and serue it. [A Noble Boke off Cookry (England, 1468)]

> Cawdelle ferry. To mak cawdelle ferry, tak clene yolks of egge welle betene and in the betyng do away the scome then put

them in a pot with swet wyne and stirr hem well all to gedure and alay it with bred of payn mayne stept in swete wyne and boile it and put sugure ther to and colour it with saffron and salt it and at the first boile set it from the fyere then dres it in lesks iij or iiij in a dyshe and cast on sugur and serue it. [A Noble Boke off Cookry (England, 1468)]

To mak cawdelle fferrens, tak hennys parboiled and conys and chop them and put them in a pot with swet brothe of beef and set it to the fyere and put ther to clowes mace pynes and raissins of corrans put ther to a litille wyne and colour it with saffron, and it be to xmesse tak the yolks of xl eggs well bet and do away the streyne then tak canelle and sanders mellide with som licour and draw it through a cloth and put it into the pot and tak half a pound of pouder of guinger and put it to the egg at the setting doune and stirre it to geddure and mak thy pot rynyinge and somdele honging and serue it. [A Noble Boke off Cookry (England, 1468)]

The first one calls for almond milk but leaves out the eggs, and the second has the final dish being so thick it can be sliced. The third calls for meat and other diverse ingredients and doesn't seem to be similar at all.

Of all the many versions of caudel ferry, the *Wagstaff* version appears to be unique in mentioning specific kinds of wine.

85. Charlet
There are two recipes for Charlet in *A Noble Boke off Cookry*, and while the first one below (recipe 191) is closest to the *Wagstaff* recipe, both seem to leave out the second half of the recipe.

To mak charlet tak swet mylk and colour it with saffron then tak freche pork and boile it and hew yt smalle then swinge eggs and cast them into the mylk and boile them and stirr them lest they bren and bete it with a litill ale and set it doun and let it not be brown and serue it. [A Noble Boke off Cookry (England, 1468)]

To mak charlet tak freche porke and sethe it and swing eggs ther withe then hewe the pork smalle and boile it in swet mylk and serue it. [A Noble Boke off Cookry (England, 1468)]

The two versions of Charlet in *Two Fifteenth-Century Cookery-Books* however are clearly different versions of the *Wagstaff* recipe.

Charlete. Capitulum Clxxviij. Seth melke yn a pott and cast ther-to salt and saffron; and hew feyre buttes of calues or of porke small, and cast ther-to: and draw the white and yolkes of eyren, and cast to the licour when it builleth, and a litell ale, and stirre it till it crudde. and yiffe thou wilt haue it forced, hete milke scaldyng hoote, and cast ther-to rawe yolkes of eyren and poudre of gyngeuere, and sugre and clowes and maces, and lete natt fully buille; and press the cruddes in feyre lenyn cloth, and lessh it, and ley too or thre lesshes in a dissh: and cast the farsyng ther-on, and serue it forth hote. [Two Fifteenth-Century Cookery-Books (England, 1430)]

lvj - Charlette. Take Mylke, an caste on a potte, with Salt and Safroun y-now; than hewe fayre buttys of Calf or of Porke, no3t to fatte, alle smal, an kaste ther-to; than take Eyroun, the whyte an the 3olke, and draw thorw a straynoure; an whan the lycoure ys in boyling, caste ther-to thin Eyroun and Ale, and styre it tylle it Crodde; than presse it a lytil with a platere, an serue forth; saue, caste ther-on brothe of Beeff or of Capoun. [Two Fifteenth-Century Cookery-Books (England, 1430)]

86. Perys in confyte
There is a version of Pears in Confit in Forme of Cury, but it is decidedly different than the *Wagstaff* version.

PEERES IN CONFYT. XX.VI. XII. Take peeres and pare hem clene. take gode rede wyne & mulberes oþer saundres and seeþ þe peeres þerin & whan þei buth ysode, take hem up, make a syryp of wyne greke. oþer vernage with blaunche powdour oþer white sugur and powdour gyngur & do the peres þerin. seeþ it a lytel & messe it forth. [Forme of Cury (England, 1390)]

87. Perys in composte

This recipe is a close match to recipe 180 in *A Noble Boke off Cookry*. Curiously, the Noble version accidentally left out the wine at the start.

> To mak peres in composte tak a good quantite of canelle and sugur and set it on the fyer to boile and draw yt throughe a stren then lesk dates thyn and put them ther to in a pot and boille wardens and pair them and put them in the ceripe put ther to sanders and boile them and alay them up with chardwins and salt it and mak yt doucet and chargaunt and put it out of the vesselle in to a treene vesselle and let it boille then pare smalle raisins and tried guinger and temper it ij dais or ij nyghtes with wyne then lay it in clarified hony cold a day and nyght then tak the raisins out of the hony and cast ther to peres in composte and serue it furthe with a cold ceripe. [A Noble Boke off Cookry (England, 1468)]

There are also two versions of this recipe in *Two Fifteenth-Century Cookery-Books*.

> Perys en Composte. Take Wyne an Canel, and a gret dele of Whyte Sugre, an set it on the fyre and hete it hote, but let it nowt boyle, an draw it thorwe a straynoure; than take fayre Datys, an pyke owt the stonys, an leche hem alle thinne, an caste ther-to; thanne take Wardonys, an pare hem and sethe hem, an leche hem alle thinne, and caste ther-to in-to the Syryppe: thanne take a lytil Sawnderys, and caste ther-to, an sette it on the fyre; an ȝif thow hast charde quynce, caste ther-to in the boyling, an loke that it stonde wyl with Sugre, an wyl lyid wyth Canel, an caste Salt ther-to, an let it boyle; an than caste yt on a treen vessel, and lat it kele, and serue forth. [Two Fifteenth-Century Cookery-Books (England, 1430)]

> Peris in compost. Take Wyne, canell, And a grete dele of white Sugur, And sette hit ouer the fire, And hete hit but a litull, and noȝt boyle; And drawe hit thorgh a streynour; And then take faire dates, and y-take oute the stones, and leche hem in faire gobettes al thyn, and cast there-to; And then take pere Wardones, and pare hem, And seth hem, And leche hem in

faire gobettes, and pike oute the core, and cast hem to the Syryppe; And take a litull Saundres, and caste there-to in the boylyng, And loke that hit stonde well, with Gynger, Sugur, And well aley hit with canell, and cast salt thereto, and lete boyle; And then caste it oute in a treyn vessell, And lete kele; And then pare clene rasinges of ginger, and temper hem ij. or iij. daies, in wyne, And after, ley hem in clarefied hony colde, all a day or a night; And then take the rasons4 oute of the hony, And caste hem to the peres in composte; And then serue hit forth with sirippe, all colde, And nought hote. [Two Fifteenth-Century Cookery-Books (England, 1430)]

88. Perys in Syrup

This recipe is most like the following one for wardens in syrup from *Two Fifteenth-Century Cookery-Books*. The basic ingredients, steps, and spicing are all there. The *Wagstaff* recipe's optional addition of dates and currants makes it more like the "pears in compost" recipes.

> x - Wardonys in syryp. Take wardonys, an caste on a potte, and boyle hem till they ben tender; than take hem vp and pare hem, an kytte hem in to pecys; take y-now of powder of canel, a good quantyte, an caste it on red wyne, an draw it thorw a straynour; caste sugre ther-to, an put it in an erthen pot, an let it boyle: an thanne caste the perys ther-to, an let boyle to-gederys, an whan they haue boyle a whyle, take pouder of gyngere an caste therto, an a lytil venegre, an a lytil safron; an loke that it be poynaunt an dowcet. [Two Fifteenth-Century Cookery-Books (England, 1430)]

89. Brawn ryal brawn sypres brawn bruse

This recipe is actually several recipes combined, and is by far one of the longest I've seen in a medieval cookbook. It appears to be a slightly wordier version of recipe 177 from *A Noble Boke off Cookry*.

> To mak braun rialle tak and boille freche braun in faire water till it be som dele tender then tak blanched almondes and grind them and draw them up with som of the sam brothe and apart

of wyne as hoot as ye may then mak the mylk hot and do the braun in the strener hot and drawe it with the mylk het, put ther to grece and venyger and set it on the fyere to boile and salt it and put it in a vesselle and when it is cold take it out or chauf the vesselle with out with hoote water or againste the fyere and when ye haue it out cutt it in thyn shyves and lay iij lesks in a disshe aftur the quantite and tak pouder of guinger or pared guinger mynced with annes in comfettes and ye may draw it with som of the same with a parte of the wyne or els thou may cutt it in lesks and serue it furthe, or els ye may tak it into another colour what ye wille, and ye will haue it grene draw it with mylk of almondes and grind leke leves in a mortair and put ther to saffron and when it is ground myche or litille coloure it ther with, when ye tak it from the fyere and do as ye did the tother tym and ye may do ther to a quantite of canelle guinger or sanders and mak it broun and serue it furthe, or els ye may tak turn sole and wesshe it and wringe it well in wyn that ye sesson it up with, and when it is boiled colour it up blew or sangwene whedur ye wille and do ther with as ye did be for, or when ye tak it from the fyer and hath bene sessoned then tak freche braune sodyn tender and cutt it in thyn lesks or dice smalle and cast it into the pot and stirre it welle to gedure then put it unto another vesselle and when it is cold leshe it and serue it. [A Noble Boke off Cookry (England, 1468)]

90. Brawn ryall

This recipe, a sort of mock eggs for serving in lent, is a clear match for recipe 33 from *A Noble Boke off Cookry*.

To make braun ryall in Lent tak sownds of stok fishe dry and do them in water iij daies and chaunge the watter euerie daie tak theme up and lay them upon a bord and scrape them clene with the bak of your knyf and weshe them and sethe them in water then tak them up and sethe them in freshe fishe brothe and put to eles for to amend the brose then tak blanched almondes grond and draw them with the sam brothe bete and ye wille ye may mak ther of almaner of braun as ye did of fleshe also tak eggs, and breke a hole in the gret ende and put out the mete and washe them and dry them and set them in salt upryght and luk it be sessoned then put in som of the whit braun and som of the same braun cold and colour it with saffron and put it in pepyns as gret as an egge and fill them up / and when they be cold pull of the shelle and set them in salt and pricke it with clowes iiij or viij aboue and fill up the crown with blanche pouder and serue it furthe insted of eggs / and in the sam manner do with pouder of guinger and chaunge the colour and cutt it in gret peeces and serue it furthe as ye do braun. [A Noble Boke off Cookry (England, 1468)]

There is another version in Ancient Cookery (MS. Arundel 334) that is more descriptively titled "jellied eggs".

Eyren Gelide. Take mylk of lib of almondes drawen up thik, and set hit over the fire, and put therto sugre, and when hit is boyled, set' hit on fide ; and then take foundes of stokfysshe, and of codlygne, and one gobet of thornbag, and fethe hom altogedur; and .when hit is fothern, thricche oute the water, and bray hit, and in the brayinge alay hit with the fame mylk, and cast therto clowes; and when hit is brayed, draw hit thik thurgh a straynour, and hete hit over the fire. And take eyren avoided al oute that is therin, and save the zolkes als hole as thow may (as whole as you can), and washe hom clene; and then put in the stuff als hote in the fhelles, and take clowes, and gilde the heddes, and plant hom aboven there hit is voyde, and set hom upright; and when the stuff is colde, pille away the shelles, and take leches lumbard cut on leches, and lay hit in chargeburs, and strawe above pouder of ginger, and sugre, medeled togeder; . then set the eyren betwene, and serve hit forthe. [Arundel 334 (England, 1425)]

91. Betrayn yn lentyn

This recipe is almost identical to recipe 34 in *A Noble Boke off Cookry*.

To mak Breteyne in Lent tak braun that is mad in lent put ther to poudur of pepper pouder of clowes and cannelle a good dele of sanders then tak blanched almondes diced in a parte of wyne and a part of vinygar and put it to gedur in a pot and when it is boiled put it into another vesselle and when it is cold leshe it and serue it as ye did braun ryalle. [A Noble Boke off Cookry (England, 1468)]

92. Betreyn in flesch tyme
This recipe is a match for recipe 35 in *A Noble Boke off Cookry*.

To mak Bretyn in fleshe tym tak calves feet skald them and sethe them in wyne and a part of swet brothe till they be tender then tak them upe and lay them upon a bord and pik out the bones and chope them all to gedure and tempere them up with the sam brothe and put them into the pot and dice the synuks then tak blanched almonde pouder of pepper and pouder of clowes a gret dele and meld alitill pouder of cannelle and sanders and saffron and set them on the fyere and when it comethe put ther to yolks of eggs diced smalle pouder of guinger venyegar and salt and put it in a small vessell and when it is cold leshe it and serue it. [A Noble Boke off Cookry (England, 1468)]

It is notable that along with the previous recipe, "Betrayn yn lentyn", I could not find this pair of recipes in any source other than *Wagstaff* and *Noble*.

93. Storgeon for sopers
This recipe is a match for recipe 36 from *A Noble Boke off Cookry*.

To mak sturgion for sopers tak calves feet the hert and the lung soden tender then hewe them and temper them up with the same brothe and ye may grond them and strawe on foilis of parsly poudre of pepper guinger clowes and salt and boile it and lay it on a clene bord and kepe it well to gedure that it run not abrod and when it is cold cutt it in iij lesks then put venygar in a bolle and mynte onyons parsly and pouder of guinger and lay the leskes ther in and serue iij or iiij in a dyshe and som of the sauce poured on. [A Noble Boke off Cookry (England, 1468)]

The recipe is a bit unusual in that it has both fish-day and meat-day aspects (sturgeon and calf, respectively) which lead me to wonder if the inclusion of calf's feet was a copy error.

94. Cold lech viaund

This recipe is a match for recipe 37 from *A Noble Boke off Cookry*, making the fifth recipe in sequence in both sources.

> To mak cold lesche vyand, tak quynces boiled paire them and pik out the core and cutt them in small pesses and put them in an erthen pot put ther to whyt grec and alay them up with hony claryfied and with raw yolks of egges and a littil almonde mylk and dates pouder of saffron and lesche it furthe. [A Noble Boke off Cookry (England, 1468)]

The word "buyst" in the *Wagstaff* version is given here as "core". I suspect it was meant as the Middle-English word "buiste" or "boist", meaning box or socket, possibly from the French "bois" (wood).

95. Lech lumbard

There is a recipe for Leche Lombard in *A Noble Boke off Cookry* (recipe 22), but it seems to be missing the a portion at the beginning.

> Lesk Lombard. Boile gadur of the skome and set it to the fyere agayne put ther to pouder of pepper canelle and grated bred and stirre it well to gedur colour it withe saffron and sanders and in the settinge doun do ther to a litill venygar mellid with pouder of guinger and stirr it and let it be stif then gadur it up in a clothe and splat it some dele abrod and couer it with the same clothe till it be colde and lay ij or iij lesks in a dyshe and straw ther on pouder of guinger mellid with sugur and serue it. [A Noble Boke off Cookry (England, 1468)]

There are several other recipes with the same title in surviving cookbooks, but most include ingredients like dates or pork that would make for a very different final product. The closest to the *Wagstaff* version is the following one from Ancient Cookery.

> Leche lumbarde. Take honey clarified, and vernage, or other wyne, and let hit boyle togeder, and colour hit with faundres and saffron, and cast therto pouder of pepur, or of greynes, and a lytel pouder of canel, and in the boylynge cast therto grated bred to make hit thik; and when hit is sul boyled, that hit be thik ynogh in the fettynge doune, put therto a lytel vynegur, medelet; with pouder of ginger, and stere hit togeder; and then poure al on a faire canevas, and let hit'kele; and when hit is colde, cut hit in faire brode leches, and lay hom in dishes, and strawe above sugre, and pouder of ginger medeled togeder; and serve hit forth. [Arundel 334 (England, 1425)]

96. Cold bruet of rabets

This recipe is a match for recipe 38 in *A Noble Boke off Cookry*.

> To mak cold bruet for rabettes tak and grind raissines or dates and drawe them up with ossay put ther in creme of almonds and pouder of cannelle a good quantite drawen with swet wyne and with pouder lombard pouder of guinger venygar and sugur then sett it on the fyere and when it is at boilinge tak it doun and put it in a bole then tak a rabet and boile it in good brothe then tak hym up and unlace hym by the bak from the bones on bothe sides and lay them in the sewe and when ye serue them furthe chop them in peces and raise the wings and leggs of chekkins and kerue them hole and chop the bodis and put them in the sewe and serue them furthe in the manner of sewe ryalle or egre douce. [A Noble Boke off Cookry (England, 1468)]

There are other recipes for rabbit stew in medieval cookbooks, but I haven't seen any with this combination of ingredients.

Based on a comparison of the two versions, I believe that the word "qyall" in *Wagstaff* is a copy error of "ryalle" (royal).

97. Dyvers desire

This monster of a recipe appears to be several (ten?) recipes in one, and while individual pieces are similar to recipes in other sources the recipe as a whole seems to be unique.

98. Viaund ryall

There is a recipe for viand royal in Ancient Cookery, but it bears only a passing resemblance to the recipe in *Wagstaff*.

> Viande riall for xl. mees. Take a galone of vernage, and fethe hit into iii. quartes, and take a pynte therto, and two pounde of sugree, ii. lb. of chardekoynes (qu. cardamums), a pounde of pasteroiale, and let hit fethe untyl a galone of vernage. Take the yolkes of 60 eyren, and bete hom togeder, and drawe hom thurgh a straynour, and in the fettynge doune of the fyre putte the zolkes therto, and a pynte of water of ewrose, and a quartrone of pouder of gynger, and dresse hit in dysshes plate, and take a barre of golde soy le, and another of fylver foyle, and laye hom on Seint Andrews croffe wysc above the potage; and then take sugre plate or gynger plate, or paste royale, and kutte hom of losenges, and plante hom in the voide places betwene the barres; and serve hit forthe. [Ancient Cookery (England, 1425)]

99. Mawmene ryall

There is a recipe for mawmeny in *A Noble Boke off Cookry* that has some of the elements of this recipe, but it is nowhere near as detailed.

> To mak mamony, tak whit wyne and sugur then bray the braun of viii capons with a gal on of oile and a quart of hony put ther to poudur of pepper galingalle guingere and canelle and stirre it welle and serue it. [A Noble Boke off Cookry (England, 1468)]

Other sources have mawmeny recipes that are closer to the *Wagstaff* version. The two below are similar in detail, with the one from *Two Fifteenth-Century Cookery-Books* being the best match.

Mawmenee. XX. Take a pottel of wyne greke. and ii. pounde of sugur take and clarifye the sugur with a qantite of wyne an drawe it thurgh a straynour in to a pot of erthe take flour of Canell. and medle with sum of the wyne an cast to gydre. take pynes with Dates and frye hem a litell in grece oþer in oyle and cast hem to gydre. take clowes an flour of canel hool and cast þerto. take powdour gyngur. canel. clower, colour it with saundres a lytel yf hit be nede cast salt þerto. and lat it seeþ; warly with a slowe fyre and not to thyk, take brawn of Capouns yteysed. oþer of Fesauntes teysed small and cast þerto. [Forme of Cury (England, 1390)]

Mawmene. Take vernage, or other strenger wyne of the best that a man may finde, and put hit in a potte, and cast there-to a gode quantite of powder Canell, And sette hit ouer the fire, And yif hit a hete; And then wring oute softe thorgh a streynour, that the draff go not oute, And put in a faire potte; take and pike newe faire pynes, And wassh hem clene in wyne, And caste of hem a grete quantite there-to; And take white sugur ynowe, as moche as thi licour is, And cast there-to; and take confeccions or charge de quyns, a goode quantite, and cast thereto; and drawe a few saundres with stronge wyne thorgh a Streynour, and cast there to; And put al in a potte; And cast there-to a good quantite of Clowes, and sette hit ouer the fire, and gif hit a boyling; And take Almondes, and drawe hem with mighti wyne thorgh a streynour; And at the first boiling, a-ley hit vp, and yeve hit a boyle; and ley hit vp with ale, and gif hit a boyle, and sette hit fro the fire; and caste thereto tesid brawne of Fesaunte, partrich, or capon, a good quantite, and ceson hit vppe with pouder of ginger ynogh, and a litull saffron and salt; And if hit be stronge, aley hit with vinegre of swete wyn, and dresse hit flatte with the bak of a Saucer or A ladell; And as thou dressest hit with the saucer in vinegre or mighty wyne, wete the saucer or ladell fore cleving, and loke that hit haue sugur right ynogh, And serve hit forth. [Two Fifteenth-Century Cookery-Books (England, 1430)]

100. Gely on fysch days

There is a recipe for fish jelly in *A Noble Boke off Cookry*, but the wording and instructions are very different.

> To mak tenche in gilly put red wyn in a pan then skald the tenche and splat him and cast hym into the panne and sethe hym and when he is enoughe lay hym in a plater and pill of the skyn and pik out the bones then set the licour and the skyn to the fyere and put ther to sugur to mak it doucet but ye may not put in the sugar till they two have boiled then cast in saffron salt ginger and vergius and let it renne throughe a strene and lay your tenche in a platter and plant hyme with blanched almondes and put on the gilly and serue it. [A Noble Boke off Cookry (England, 1468)]

The fish jelly recipes from other sources describe much the same process, but again with different wording.

> GELE OF FYSSH. C. I. Take Tenches, pykes, eelys, turbut and plays, kerue hem to pecys. scalde hem & waische hem clene. drye hem with a cloth do hem in a panne do þerto half vyneger & half wyne & seeþ it wel. & take the Fysshe and pike it clene, cole the broth thurgh a cloth into a erthen panne. do þerto powdour of pep and safroun ynowh. lat it seeþ and skym it wel whan it is ysode dof grees clene, cowche fisshes on chargeours & cole the sewe thorow a cloth onoward & serue it forth. [Forme of Cury (England, 1390)]

> Cx - Gelye de Fysshe. Take newe Pykys, an draw hem, and smyte hem to pecys, and sethe in the same lycoure that thou doste Gelye of Fleysshe; an whan they ben y-now, take Perchys and Tenchys, and sethe; and Elys, an kutte hem in fayre pecys, and waysshe hem, and putte hem in the same lycoure, and loke thine lycoure be styf y-now; and ȝif it wolle notte cacche, (Note: stick; see other Cookery, No. 174) take Soundys of watteryd Stokkefysshe, or ellys Skynnys, or Plays, an caste ther-to, and sethe ouer the fyre, and skeme it wyl; and when it ys y-now, let nowt the Fysshe breke; thenne take the lycoure fro the fyre, and do as thou dedyst be (Note: By, with) that other Gelye, saue, pylle the Fysshe, and ley ther-off in dysshis, that is,

perche and suche; and Flowre hem, and serue forthe. [Two Fifteenth-Century Cookery-Books (England, 1430)]

It is worth noting that the recipes from *Wagstaff* and *Noble* appear to be the only fish jelly recipes that call for almonds.

101. Cristell gely

This recipe is in part almost identical to recipe 39 in *A Noble Boke off Cookry*.

> To mak cristalle gilly tak whyt wyne that will hold hir colour and boil the fishe ther in and let it stand and serve it furthe. [A Noble Boke off Cookry (England, 1468)]

102. Gely of flesch

This recipe appears to be a match to recipe 40 in *A Noble Boke off Cookry*, though the *Wagstaff* version is missing some of the detail.

> To mak a gilly of fleshe take conys and fley them and skald pegions chop them and fley of the skyne skald chekins and chope kiddes and put all to gedur and boile it in red wyne then tak it upe and lay it in a clene clothe dry the peces of the kid pigions and conys and couche them in dishe and chope chekkins and put ther to then set the chekkins in a cold place where it may stand stille then set the brothe to the fyere agayne and luk it be well strened that no fat abid ther on then tak skalded caluys feet and lay them in the same brothe till they be tender and luk the brothe be clene scomed sessen it up with salt and serue it. [A Noble Boke off Cookry (England, 1468)]

It is worth noting that, of all the surviving recipes for meat gelatin, these two appear to be the only ones that call for such a variety of meat but do not call for adding spices like saffron or cinnamon.

103. Creme of almondys

This recipe appears to be a match to recipe 41 in *A Noble Boke off Cookry*.

To mak creme of almonds tak blanched almondes and grind
them up and temper them up akurd thik mylk with faire water
drawe it into the pot and sett it on the fyere and stirre it welle
when it begynnethe to rise / and ye have to myche put ther to
a dishefulle of venygar if ther be alitille putt ther in the lesse
hille the pot and let it stand awhile then tak a clene cloth and
hold it abrod betweene iiij men strait cast the creme there in
and rube it undirnethe the clothe with a ladille toward and
froward with the egge of the ladille to draw out the watter then
gadur it to gedur unto the myddle of the clothe then bind the
corners to gedur and hong it upon a pyne and let the water run
out then put it in a bolle and temper it up withe wyne and
bruse it with a saucer as soft as ye wille and serue it. [A Noble
Boke off Cookry (England, 1468)]

There are very similar recipes in other contemporary sources,
including the direction beginning with "if you have much", which
suggests that this was a popular recipe of the time.

Creme of Almonds. Recipe & blawnch almondes, & grinde
þam & kepe þam als whyte as ȝe mey, & temper it thyk with
watur & draw it, & put it in a pott. And sett it oure þe fyre &
styr it wele; and when it begyns to rise take it of. If ȝe wyll haue
mykyll, þan do a lityll þerto of vinegre & lat it stande a whyle,
& take a clene cloth haldyn abrode betwene tiw men, & trast
þerin with a ladyl als brode as þe cloth wyll striche towards &
froward ay with þe ege of þe ladyll þat ȝe may draw oute all þe
watyrs; & þan gedyre it to þe corners togydyrs & hang it vpon
a pyn, & let þe water soke oute into a boll; & temper it with
whyte wyne, & bruse it with a sawcer tyll it be als softe as ȝe
wyll haue it, & serof it forth. [MS Harley 5401 (England, 15th
century)]

To make Creme of Almoundes. Blanche almounds kepe them
As ye may them temper up to A thycke mylke with fayre water
streyne hit and put hit in A pott and set hit on the fyre stere hit
well when hit begynnys to ryse up take hit of yf thow have
moche do ther to A dyschfull of VynAgyr yf thou have but a
litell do the lesse hele the pot let hit stonde A whyle. Take a
clene cloth holdyn a brode betwene .iiij. folkes streyte & cast

the creme þer on with a ladyll as brode as the cloth And rubbe the cloth toward and froward with the egge of the ladyll that þer may woyde the water. Then gather hit to geder in þe myddyl of the cloth bynde the .iiij. Corners to geder and hang on A pynne that the Water may soke onto And then do hit in A bolle And tempyr hit up wyth white wyne And bete hit with a sawser on to the tyme that hit be softe. [MS Pepys 1047 (England, ca. 1500)]

104. Hages of Almayne

This recipe is a close match for recipe 42 from *A Noble Boke off Cookry*.

To mak an hagges of Almayne tak and draw eggs through a strener and parboile parcely in fat brothe then hew it and hew yolks of eggs to gedure put ther to pouder of guinger sugur and salt. and put mary in a strene and let it honge in the pot boilling and parboille it and tak it upe and let it kele then cutt it smalle and tak egg drawen throughe a strener and put them into a pan and let the pan be moist of grece let the batter ryn abrod into a foile then couche ther in iij hard yolks of eggs and mary and parsly and turn the iiij sides to gedur that they close to gedur aboue that they lie square then tak of the same bater and whit of egge that it hold stanche and close it and serue yt. [A Noble Boke off Cookry (England, 1468)]

Haggis of Almayn seems to have been a popular recipe as there are nearly identical versions in contemporary sources.

1 - Hagas de Almaynne. Take Fayre Eyroun, the ʒolke and the Whyte, and draw hem thorw a straynour; than take Fayre Percely, and parboyle it in a potte with boyling brothe; than take the ʒolkys of Eyroun hard y-sothe, and hew the ʒolkys and the Percely smal to-gederys; than take Sugre, pouder Gyngere, Salt, and caste ther-to; then take merow, and putte it on a straynourys ende, and lat hange in-to a boyling potte; and parboyle it, and take it vppe, and let it kele, and than kytte it in smal pecys; than take the drawyn Eyroun, and put hem in a panne al a-brode, and vnnethe ony grece in the panne, and

cowche ye ʒolkys and the Percely ther-on in the panne, and than cowche of the Marow pecys ther-on, and than fold vppe eche kake by-nethe eche corner in .iiij. square, as platte, and turne it on the panne oneʒ; let lye a litel whyle; than take it vp and serue forth. [Two Fifteenth-Century Cookery-Books (England, 1430)]

Hagas de almondes. Take faire yolkes of eyren, and the White, and drawe hem thorgh a Streynour, and take faire parcelly, and parboyle hit in a potte, and parboylingge brothe; And then take yolkes of yren, sodde hard, and hewe the yolkes and the parcely small togidre; And take sugur, pouder of Gynger, and salte, and cast to yolkes and parcelly; And take mary, and put hit in a streynour, And lete hong yn to the boyling potte, and parboile; and take hit vppe, and lette hit kele, And kutte hit then in smale peces; And then take the drawen eyren, and putte hem in a pan al a-brode, (And vnneth eny grece in the pan,) and couche the yolkes and the parcelly there-on in the pan. And then couche the peces of the mary thereon; And then folde vp the kake byneth euery corner, to eche corner foure square al flatte, And turne hit on the pan; And lete hit lye awhile, And then take it vp, and serue hit forth. [Two Fifteenth-Century Cookery-Books (England, 1430)]

To make a Haggas of Almain. Take two Buts of Mutton, and frye them well from Skinnes and senowes, and mince it with suet as small as you can, then take Dates and mince them smal, then take these Spices which follow, one ounce of Corance clean washed, an ounce of Ginger and asmuch of pepper, and an ounce of Sugar with the yolkes of eight or nine Egs, clean fryed from the whites. Take also fine faire light bread grated, with a little Salt, and a portion of Saffron, and boile al these togither, then row these Corance in Suet of a Calfe or Sheepe, then put them into a frying pan, and so set them into a hot oven, and when they be brown turne them, and when they be baked, take them out and serve three in a dish. [A Book of Cookrye (England, 1591)]

While the word "Almayn" in the recipe title is undoubtedly a reference to Germany ("Almagne" in French), one of the recipes in

Two Fifteenth-Century Cookery-Books takes it to mean "almonds". This is especially amusing seeing that almonds are not included among the ingredients.

105. Quystes

This recipe is a match for recipe 43 from *A Noble Boke off Cookry*.

> To mak quystis tak a pece of beef or of moton and wyne and water and boile it and scem it clene then stop the quistes within with whole peppur and cast them in a pot and cover it and let it stewe welle put ther to poudur of guinger watire and salt and cast ther to and put them in faire disches one or ij in a dische for a maner of potage and when they be serued furthe tak alitill brothe and put in the disches among the quystis and serue it. [A Noble Boke off Cookry (England, 1468)]

There is also a version of this recipe in *Two Fifteenth-Century Cookery-Books* as well.

> xiiij - Quystis Scune. Take a pece of beef or of mutoun, and wyne and fayre water, and caste in-to a potte, an late hem boyle, an skeme it wyl an clene; than take quystes, an stoppe hem wyth-in wyth hole pepyr, and marwe, an than caste hem in-to the potte, an ceuere wyl the potte, an let hem stere ry3th wyl to-gederys; an than take powder gyngere, and a lytel verious an salt, and caste ther-to, an thanne serue hem forth in a fayre dysshe, a quyste or to in a dysshe, in the maner of a potage: an whan thowe shalt serue hem forth, take a lytil of the broth, an put on dysshe wyth quystys, an serue forth. [Two Fifteenth-Century Cookery-Books (England, 1430)]

The word "quystes" in Middle English is a corruption of the Scottish word "cushat", which is a wood pigeon.

106. Vontes

This recipe is a close match for recipe 44 from *A Noble Boke off Cookry*.

To mak votose tak gobettes of mary and dates cutt gret sugur and poudur of guinger saffron and salt and mak afoile as ye did be for and do it out of the pot and mak another then tak the for said stuf and couche ther in almost as brod as the foile and wet the bredes of the foille aboue and closse it and bak it essely and when it is bak cutt it in peces eury pece ij enche square. [A Noble Boke off Cookry (England, 1468)]

107. Bastons
This recipe is a close match for recipe 45 from *A Noble Boke off Cookry*.

To mak rostand tak and mak a stiff bater of egg and pured floure sugur a goodelle and alitill yest of new ale and set it by the fier or els in a pot with boillinge watur that it may take alitile heet when it riseth swinge it to gedur and let it fall agayne and let the ovene be heet and clene swept and put the floure in an ovone to bak that it ryse as frenche bred then tak it out and cut away the cruste about the brod of a noble and mak a hole and raise it all about under the cruste and longe and ouer thwart as thyk as thou may with a knyf and so doun to the botom hole the crust all about set on the crust aboue and set them in the ovene till they be somdele dried and serue it furthe. [A Noble Boke off Cookry (England, 1468)]

There are also two versions of the same recipe in *Two Fifteenth-Century Cookery-Books* which describe the process much more clearly.

xxv - Rastons. Take fayre Flowre, and the whyte of Eyroun, and the 3olke, a lytel; than take Warme Berme, and putte al thes to-gederys, and bete hem to-gederys with thin hond tyl it be schort and thikke y-now, and caste Sugre y-now ther-to, and thenne lat reste a whyle; than kaste in a fayre place in the oven, and late bake y-now; and then with a knyf cutte yt round a-boue in maner of a crowne, and kepe the cruste that thou kyttyst; and than pyke al the cromys withynne to-gederys, an pike hem smal with thin knyf, and saue the sydys and al the cruste hole with-owte; and than caste ther-in clarifiyd Boter, and Mille the crome3 and the botere to-gedere3, and keuere it a-3en with the cruste, that thou kyttest a-way; than putte it in the ovyn a3en a lytil tyme; and than take it out, and serue it forth.

Rastons. Take fyne floure, and white of eyren, and a litul of the yolkes; And then take warme berm, and put al thes togidre, and bete hem togidre with thi honde so longe til hit be short and thik ynogh. And caste sugur ynowe thereto; And then lete rest a while; And then cast hit in a faire place in an oven, and lete bake ynogh; And then kut hit with a knyfe rownde aboue in maner of a crowne, and kepe the crust that thou kuttest, and pile all the cremes within togidre; and pike hem small with thi knyfe, and saue the sides and al the cruste hole withoute; And then cast thi clarefied butter, and medle the creme and the buttur togidre, And couer hit ayen with the cruste that thou kuttest awey; and then put hit in the oven ayen a litull tyme, and take it oute, and serue hit forthe all hote.

108. Samatays
This recipe is a close match for recipe 46 in *A Noble Boke off Cookry*.

To mak samartard tak wetted cruddes er they bee pressed and put them in a clothe and grinde them well to pured flour and temper hem with eggs and cowe creme and mak ther of a good batere that it be rynynge then, tak whit grece in a pan and let it be hete and tak out the batter with a saucer and let it ryn into the grece and draw your hand bakward that it may ryn abrod then fry it welle and whit and somwhat craking and serue it furthe in dishes with sugur ther on. [A Noble Boke off Cookry (England, 1468)]

The title of the recipe, along with some of the ingredients, leads me to think it is related to the recipe for Sambocade.

SAMBOCADE. XX.VIII. XI. Take and make a Crust in a trape. & take a cruddes and wryng out þe wheyze. and drawe hem þurgh a straynour and put in þe straynour crustes. do þerto sugur the þridde part & somdel whyte of Ayrenn. &

shake þerin blomes of elren. & bake it up with curose & messe it forth. [Forme of Cury (England, 1390)]

109. Long Fryturys

This recipe is a match for recipe 47 in *A Noble Boke off Cookry*.

To mak longe fritturs tak som of the same batter and let none other ther in for it will be the more stiff then lay it on a clene bord that is no brodder than the hond and tak the bone of a ribe of a beste and wet it in grece that the batter cleve not ther on then strik of the bater with a bone in to the pan that it may fall in smalle peces euye fritur a hand full longe serue them hot and strawe ther on sugur and ye may grind thes in the sam manner and ye will tak pork sodden tender and grind therin and mak pilottes as gret as an egge that is called fritture lombard and serue it.   [A Noble Boke off Cookry (England, 1468)]

There are also two related recipes in *Two Fifteenth-Century Cookery-Books*.

xlvj - Longe Fretoure. Take Milke, an make fayre croddes ther-of, in the maner of a chese al tendyr; than take owt the whey as clene as thou may, and putte it on a bolle; than take ȝolkys of Eyroun and Ale, and menge floure, and cast ther-to, a gode quantyte, and draw it thorw a straynoure in-to a fayre vesselle; than take a panne with fayre grece, and hete it on the fyre, but lat it nowt boyle, and than ley thin creme a-brode; than take a knyff, and kytte a quantyte ther-of fro the borde in-to the panne, and efte a-nother, and let it frye; and whan it is brownne, take it vppe in-to a fayre dyssche, and caste Sugre y-now ther-on, and serue forth.   [Two Fifteenth-Century Cookery-Books (England, 1430)]

Longe Frutours. Take Mylke And make faire croddes there-of in maner of chese al tendur, and take oute the way clene; then put hit in a faire boll, And take yolkes of egges, and white, and menge floure, and caste thereto a good quantite, and drawe hit thorgh a streynoure into a faire vessell; then put hit in a faire

pan, and fry hit a litull in faire grece, but lete not boyle; then
take it oute, and ley on a faire borde, and kutte it in faire
smale peces as thou list, And putte hem ayen into the panne
til thei be browne; And then caste Sugur on hem,
and serue hem forth. [Two Fifteenth-Century Cookery-Books
(England, 1430)]

110. Payn purdyeu

Pain perdu, known to modern English speakers as French Toast,
appears in several medieval sources. This version is a clear match
for recipe 48 from *A Noble Boke off Cookry*.

> To mak payn pardieu tak paynmayne or freshe bred and paire
> away the cruste cutt them in schyues and fry them alitill in
> clarified butter then tak yolks of eggs drawe throughe a strene
> as hot as ye may and lay the bred ther in and turn it therin that
> they be coueryd in batter and serue it and straw on sugur
> enowghe. [A Noble Boke off Cookry (England, 1468)]

There is an obvious error in the *Noble* version in that the bread is
not fried after being coated in batter.

Other versions describe pretty much the same recipe, but are
worded differently.

> xliij - Payn pur-dew. Take fayre ȝolkys of Eyroun, and trye hem
> fro the whyte, and draw hem thorw a straynoure, and take Salt
> and caste ther-to; than take fayre brede, and kytte it as
> troundeȝ rounde; than take fayre Boter that is claryfiyd, or ellys
> fayre Freysshe grece, and putte it on a potte, and make it hote;
> than take and wete wyl thin troundeȝ in the ȝolkys, and putte
> hem in the panne, an so frye hem vppe; but ware of cleuyng to
> the panne; and whan it is fryid, ley hem on a dysshe, and ley
> Sugre y-nowe ther-on, and thanne serue it forht. [Two
> Fifteenth-Century Cookery-Books (England, 1430)]

> Payn purdeuz. Take faire yolkes of eyren, and try hem fro the
> white, and drawe hem thorgh a streynour; and then take salte,
> and caste thereto; And then take manged brede or paynman,

and kutte hit in leches; and then take faire buttur, and clarefy hit, or elles take fressh grece and put hit yn a faire pan, and make hit hote; And then wete the brede well there in the yolkes of eyren, and then ley hit on the batur in the pan, whan the buttur is al hote; And then whan hit is fried ynowe, take sugur ynowe, and caste there-to whan hit is in the dissh, And so serue hit forth.   [Two Fifteenth-Century Cookery-Books (England, 1430)]

111. Ffelets of porke yn doryd

This version is a clear match for recipe 49 from *A Noble Boke off Cookry*.

To mak pestelles of pork, endored tak and broche pestellis of pork and put of the skyn and rost it then tak poudur and baist it and yolk of egge draw throughe a strener and when they be rosted dry it at the greuyng up and endor hem with yolks of eggs and serue them furthe.   [A Noble Boke off Cookry (England, 1468)]

While there are several recipes for "pommes dorre" (golden apples) in other contemporary cookbooks, these two appear unique in that the pork is not ground and formed into meatballs before cooking.

112. Hattes

This recipe is a close match for recipe 50 from *A Noble Boke off Cookry*.

To mak hattes in flesshe tyme mak a paiste of pured flour, knodene with yolks of eggs and mak a stuf of vele or pork sodene tender and ground with yolks of eggs putther to mary diced and dates mynced smalle and raissins of corrans with sugur saffron and salt and pouder mellid to gedur in paiste and wound foilles of the brod of a saucere as thyn as ye may dryf them and dryf them that the bredes may cuver to the middes of the foile then turn them to gedur that the bredes of the inor sid met all about and lesse the bred and turn upward without in the manner of an hatte and close welle the eggs that they hold

full ther in and luk the stuf haue a good batter made with yolks
of eggs and flour of whet the open sid that is downward luk
ther in that the stuf be clossed and so set it in hot grece up
right and when the battur is fried lay them doun and serve
them. [A Noble Boke off Cookry (England, 1468)]

The wording in the *Noble* version makes it clear that the incomplete
word in *Wagstaff* is "stuff". It is also interesting that the phrase
"close well the eggs" (rather than edges) is repeated in
both versions.

113. (Hattes) In lentyn
While the name "Hattes" is implicit in the title, it is explicitly
included in the corresponding recipe (number 51) in *A Noble Boke
off Cookry*.

To mak hattes in lent mak a paist of pured flour knoddene
with mylk of almondes then tak saffron eles base or molet and
the leuer of the fishe sodden and grond put them to alitille
fritture pouder of saffron and salt and mak the bater of pured
floure and almond mylk and do it as ye did be for. [A Noble
Boke off Cookry (England, 1468)]

The list of fish from the *Noble* version seems to have left out
salmon - perhaps a copying error that collapsed "saffron take fresh
salmon" into just "saffron".

114. Sauce Madam
This recipe is a close match for recipe 52 from *A Noble Boke
off Cookry*.

To mak sauce madame tak the tharmes of a gose and slit them
and shave them clene then tak the gossern the wings the skyn
and the soule of the gose and put them all in a pot with
mynced onyons mynced wardens and grapes rostid then rost
hir and smyt hir in peces and lay here in a chargiour and put
the farser in a pot put ther to wyn and sesson it up with pouder
and salt and venygar and thou wilt thou may tak yolks of egges

sodene herd and cromyd smalle and put ther to and let it be salt and pour it on the peces and serue it. [A Noble Boke off Cookry (England, 1468)]

The wording is surprisingly similar. Not only do both use of the word "tharmes/yarmazs" (entrails), but they also feature the unusual use of the pronoun "her" to describe the food in place of the more common "him" or "it".

There are versions of Sauce Madame in other surviving cookbooks, but their wording is significantly different.

> Sawse Madame. XXX. Take sawge. persel. ysope. and saueray. quinces. and peeres, garlek and Grapes. and fylle the gees þerwith. and sowe the hole þat no grece come out. and roost hem wel. and kepe the grece þat fallith þerof. take galytyne and grece and do in a possynet, whan the gees buth rosted ynowh; take an smyte hem on pecys. and þat tat is withinne and do it in a possynet and put þerinne wyne if it be to thyk. do þerto powdour of galyngale. powdour douce and salt and boyle the sawse and dresse þe Gees in disshes and lay þe sowe onoward. [Forme of Cury (England, 1390)]

> Sawce madame. Take sawge, persoly, ysope, saveray, Onyons gode, peres, garlek, I say, And grapes. go fille þy gose þenne And sew þy hole, no grece oute renne. Lay hur to fyre and rost hyr browne, And kepe þo grece þat falles doune. Take galingale and þo grece þat renne, Do hit in posnet, as I þe kenne. Whenne þo gose is rostyd, take hir away, Smyte hir in pesys, I þe pray. Þat is within, þou schalle take oute, Kest in þy posnet with outene doute. 3if hit is thyke do þerto wyne, And powder of galingale þat is fyne, And powder dowce and salt also. Boyle alle togeder er þou fyr go, In a dysshe þy gose þou close Þe sawce abofe, as I suppose. [Liber cure cocorum (England, 1430)]

> Sauce Madame. Take sauge and parsel, ysope, and saveray, and qwynses (quinces), and gode percs pared, and cut hom and garlyk and grapes; then take gees clene wasshen, and fyl the gees therwythe, and sowe wel the hole that no grees go oute,

and rost horn wel, and kepe the gresc clene that droppes in the rostynge ; then take galentyne and the grees of the gees, and do hit in a postenet (pipkin); and when the gees byn ynough, take hom of the fpitte and smyte hom on peces, and take that that is within smal hewen, and do it in the postenet; and do therto a litel wyn and raisynges of corance, and pouder of gynger and of canel, and let hit boyle, then dresse thi gees in platers, and poure the sauce above, and serve hit forthe. [Ancient Cookery (England, 1425)]

115. Sauce camelyn for quaylys & othir maner of foules and fysch
This recipe is a match for recipe 53 from *A Noble Boke off Cookry*.

To mak sauce camelyne for quaile, tak whyt bred and drawe it in the sauce in the manner of guinger sauce with venyger put ther to pouder of guinger canelle and pouder lombard a goodelle and ye may draw alitille mustard ther with and sesson it up with mustard that it be douce salt it and colour it with saffron and serue it. [A Noble Boke off Cookry (England, 1468)]

On its own, the phrase "mustard that it be douce" in the *Noble* version is odd, but the error is made clear by the substitution of "sugar" in *Wagstaff* for the second appearance of "mustard".

There are many recipes for Camaline Sauce in surviving cookbooks, with a wide variety of ingredients, but these two are the only ones I've found that call for mustard.

116. Chaudon of Swan or of wylde goose
This recipe is a match for recipe 54 from *A Noble Boke off Cookry*.

To mak chandron for swannes, tak the hert of a swan and the gossern and the tharmes and slit them and shave them and sethe them, do ther to the feet and wings mak them smalle and put them in a pot and boile it then drawe a liour of bred and red wine and alay it up then sesson it with pouder of pepper guinger and salt and let it haue a good colour of blod then tak out the smale bones of the feet and let the skyn be hole and lay a foot in a disshe and a wing there on and serue it. [A Noble Boke off Cookry (England, 1468)]

Chaudron of Swan appears to have been an popular and enduring recipe, with examples showing up in cookbooks up through the 17th century.

117. Wellyd pepyr for rostyd veele
This recipe is a close match for recipe 57 from *A Noble Boke off Cookry*.

To mak wellid peper for rost vele tak and cutt bred in schyves and toist it upon a gridirne that it be somdele broun and ye may grat it and temper it with wyne or ale and drawe it throughe a strener that it be somdele thik put ther to pouder and saffron and boile it and serue it hot but let it haue a taist of venygar. [A Noble Boke off Cookry (England, 1468)]

Simple pepper sauces for veal are reasonably common, but "Welled Pepper" appears to be unique to *Noble* and *Wagstaff*.

118. Fresch lamprey bakyn
This recipe is a match for recipe 55 from *A Noble Boke off Cookry*.

To bak a freche lampry tak and put a quyk lampry in a pot put ther to a porcyon of red wyne then stop the pot close that he lep not out and when he is dyinge tak him out and put hym in skaldinge water then tak hym in your handes with alyn clothe and a handfull of hay in the tother hand and strik hym so that the skyn go away and saue him hole then weshe hym and cut hym out whart a straw brod from the naville so that the stringe be lowse, then slitt hym a litill at the throt and tak out the string and kep the blode in a vesselle and it be a female thrust in your hand from the naville upwards so that the spawn com out ther as ye tak out the stringe and ye will boile it salt it a litill in the same place within that ye may cum and lowse the

bone with a prik from the fische and brek it a litill from the
hed and slit hym a litill from the taille then put the prik
betwene the bone and the fische and drawe the bone from the
taille as esly as ye may that it cum out all hole from the taile
then wind the bone about thy finger and drawe it out softly for
breking and so ye shall tak it out hole then chope the lampry
o[u with curl] twhart the bak eury pece iij fingers brode and let
them hold to gedure and toile them welle in the blod, and ye
will mak your galentyn of crust of white bred cutt it in schyves
and toiste it on a gredirne that it be somdelle broun and tak a
quart of good red wyne for the bakinge of the lampry and put
the bred ther in and drawe it and mak it not chargaunt and ye
will ye may grind a fewe of raissins and mak it up ther with and
let the fyft part be venygar put ther to pouder of cannelle a
gretdele, pouder galingalle pouder lombard pouder of guinger
sugur saffron and salt and let it be be tweene braun and
yallowe and mak thy colour of sanders then mak a large coffyn
of pured floure and put thy lampry ther in and put in the
galentyn that it stand as highe as the lampery and let it haue a
good lide and wet the bredes round about and lay it in the
coffyn and close it round about to the pen for ye must haue a
pen betweene the lidd and the coffyne to blow the pen that the
lid may rise welle and luk the ovene be hoot and set it in to it.
[A Noble Boke off Cookry (England, 1468)]

There is also a similar recipe in *Two Fifteenth-Century Cookery-Books*.

xxiij - Lamprays bake. Take and make fayre round cofyns of
fyne past, and take Freyssche lampreys, and late hem blode .iij.
fyngerys with-in the tayle, and lat hem blede in a vesselle, and
late hym deye in the same vesselle in the same blode; than take
broun Brede, and kyt it, and stepe it in the Venegre, and draw
thorw a straynoure; than take the same blode, and pouder of
Canel, and cast ther-to tyl it be broun; than caste ther-to
pouder Pepir, Salt, and Wyne a lytelle, that it be no3t to strong
of venegre. An skald the Lampray, and pare hem clene, and
couche hym round on the cofyn, tyl he be helyd; than kyuere
hym fayre with a lede, saue a lytel hole in the myddelle, and at
that hool, blow in the cofynne with thin mowthe a gode blast
of Wynde. And sodenly stoppe the hole, that the wynd a-byde

with-ynne, to reyse vppe the cofynne, that he falle nowt a-
dowune; and whan he is a lytel y-hardid in the ouen, pryke the
cofyn with a pynne y-stekyd on a roddys ende, for brekyng of
the cofynne, and than lat bake, and serue forth colde. And
when the lamprey is take owt of the cofynne and etyn, take the
Syrippe in the cofynne, and put on a chargere, and caste Wyne
ther-to, an pouder Gyngere, and lat boyle in the fyre. Than
take fayre Paynemayn y-wette in Wyne, and ley the soppis in
the cofynne of the lamprey, and ley the Syrippe a-boue, and ete
it so hot; for it is gode lordys mete. [Two Fifteenth-Century
Cookery-Books (England, 1430)]

119. Tartes of Flesch

This recipe is a close match for recipe 58 from *A Noble Boke
off Cookry*.

To mak tartes of fleshe tak pork and pik out the bones and
grind it smale then boile figges in the freche brothe of flesche
of wyne or of ale hewe it and grind it with egge then paire
tender ches and grind ther with and let the most part stand by
flesche then tak pynes and raissins and fry them a litille in grece
and put it to the other with hole clowes maces poudur of
pepper and cannele a goodele of guinger saffron sugur or hony
clarified then salt it and toile them welle to gedur while the
grece is hot, and mak gret coffynes with lowe liddes and ye
may strawe ther to clowes maces and mynced dates whedur ye
wille mold them with the stuf or strawe them aboue, and lay on
the liddes wild werks and endor them with mylk of almondes
and saffron and endore them as ye bak them and serue them
furthe. [A Noble Boke off Cookry (England, 1468)]

120. Tartelets

This recipe is a match for recipe 59 from *A Noble Boke off Cookry*.

To mak tartalettes, mak smalle coffins in the same manner as
ye did the tother and mak your stuf of boylled figges ground
and good powdure and spices and put ther to other fische or
fleshe and sesson it up in the same manner and fille the coffins

ther with and ye may fry them or bak them whedure ye wille and serue them. [A Noble Boke off Cookry (England, 1468)]

121. Bakyn purpays
This recipe is a match for recipe 60 from *A Noble Boke off Cookry*.

To bak porpas sturgion or turbot tak poudred porpas and parboile it welle and stripe of the skyn and tak pouder of pepper and canelle. and it be ned meld it well with the fische then close it up in the foile or paiste and bak it, and ye may tak venyson in the sam manner. [A Noble Boke off Cookry (England, 1468)]

The reference to venison is noteworthy in that porpoise was the common fish-day substitution for venison, to the point that many recipes for porpoise call for it to be served with frumenty, which is the typical side dish for venison.

122. Pyes of flesch capons and fesaunttes
This recipe is a match for recipe 61 from *A Noble Boke off Cookry*.

To mak pyes of flesche of capon or of fessand tak good beef pork vele and venison hew it smalle do ther to pork of peper clowes maces guinger and mynced dates and raissins of corans mete it with malmsey or vergius and cast in saffron and salt and luk it be welle sessoned then couch it in a large coffyne and couch in the capon or fessand hole and if ye wille smyt them in peces and colour them with saffron and put in it other wild foule if ye wille and plant ther in hard yolks of egges and strawe on clowes maces dates mynced raissins of corrans quybibes then close them up and bak them and serue them. [A Noble Boke off Cookry (England, 1468)]

The combination of capon and pheasant in a pie, along with the other meats listed, is unusual. I have not found any related recipes in other contemporary sources.

123. Crustad lumbard

This recipe is a match for recipe 62 from *A Noble Boke off Cookry*.

> To mak custad lombard mak a large coffyn then tak dates from
> the stones tak gobettes of mary and smalle birdes and parboile
> them in salt brothe and couche ther in then tak clowes mace
> and raisins of corans and pynes fryed and strawe ther on and
> sett them in the oven to bak and luk ye haue a coup of cowes
> creme yolks of eggs good pouderes saffron sanderes and salt
> then fill the coffins ther with, and on fishe daies boille wardens
> or other peres paire them and hole them at the crown then fill
> them full of blaunche poudur and torn them in blaunche
> poudur and skoche them all about that the pouder may abid
> ther in then set the stalks upryght and ye may mak your coup
> of creme of almondes and shak up your custad as ye did of
> flesche and when they be bak gilt the stalkes of the peres and
> serue them. [A Noble Boke off Cookry (England, 1468)]

There is a recipe for "Custard Lombard" in *Two Fifteenth-Century
Cookery-Books*, but the wording is significantly different.

> Custard lumbarde. Take good creme, and ffoiles of and yolkes
> And white of egges, and breke hem thereto, and streyne hem
> all thorgh a straynour till hit be so thik that it woll bere him
> self; And take faire Mary, And Dates, cutte in ij. or iij. and
> prunes, and put hem in faire coffyns of paast; And then put the
> coffyn in an oven, And lete hem bake till thei be hard, And
> then drawe hem oute, and putte the licoure into the Coffyns,
> And put hem into the oven ayen, And lete hem bake till they
> be ynogh, but cast sugur and salt in thi licour whan ye putte hit
> into the coffyns; And if hit be in lenton, take creme of
> Almondes, And leve the egges And the Mary. [Two Fifteenth-
> Century Cookery-Books (England, 1430)]

124. Chauet of Beef

This recipe is a close match for recipe 64 from *A Noble Boke
off Cookry*.

To mak chewettes of beef tak beef and cutt it smalle and do ther to pouder of guinger clowes and other good poudurs grapes vergius saffron and salt and toile them welle to gedure put chekins chopped in coffins and yolks of eggs brok smale and bak them and serue them. [A Noble Boke off Cookry (England, 1468)]

There is a similar recipe in *Two Fifteenth-Century Cookery-Books* for Chewetts, but it doesn't call for the chicken as the *Noble* and *Wagstaff* versions do.

Chawettys. Take buttys of Vele, and mynce hem smal, or Porke, and put on a potte; take Wyne, and caste ther-to pouder of Gyngere, Pepir, and Safroun, and Salt, and a lytel verthous, and do hem in a cofyn with 3olkys of Eyroun, and kutte Datys and Roysonys of Coraunce, Clowys, Mace3, and then ceuere thin cofyn, and lat it bake tyl it be y-now. [Two Fifteenth-Century Cookery-Books (England, 1430)]

125. Chauet Ryall
This recipe is a close match for recipe 66 from *A Noble Boke off Cookry*.

To mak chewettes rialle cutt mary in small peces and couche it in smale coffins with smale birdes parboiled or rabettes and dates put ther to sugur salt vergious and saffron and luk it stond welle by mary put ther to pouder of guinger and other good pouders then close them bak them and serue them. [A Noble Boke off Cookry (England, 1468)]

None of the recipes for chewetts that I could find in the other medieval sources uses this particular combination of ingredients.

126. Bakyn chikenes
This recipe is a close match for recipe 65 from *A Noble Boke off Cookry*.

To bak chekyns tak chekins clene skaldid and truse them as short as ye may colour them with saffron and salt them then couche them in coffins and take salt lard of pork and dice it smale and melleit with vergious saffron and good poudurs and couche them in coffins and close them and bak them and serue them. [A Noble Boke off Cookry (England, 1468)]

127. Chauet yn fysch dayes
This recipe is a close match for recipe 67 from *A Noble Boke off Cookry*.

To mak chewettes on fische dais tak molet freshe samon or bace rawe clef them frome the bone and chope them in peces and couche them in coffins put eles ther to and othere metes as ye did be for and mak a ceripe of thik almond mylk all saue the juce of eggs then set the coffins in the ovon and fille them fulle of good ceripe and ye may fry the fische and serue it furthe. [A Noble Boke off Cookry (England, 1468)]

128. Darrolete
This recipe is a match for recipe 68 from *A Noble Boke off Cookry*.

To mak dariolites tak mynced fisshe and almond mylk mad with wyne and mynced bred sanders saffron raissins of corans hony and pouder and mele all to gedur so that it be thik and put it in the coffyn and bak it in the manner of flawnes and serue it. [A Noble Boke off Cookry (England, 1468)]

There are numerous recipes in other sources for Dariols, but the *Wagstaff* and *Noble* versions are the only ones I've found that include minced fish.

129. Prineroll at pasche
This recipe is a match for recipe 69 from *A Noble Boke off Cookry*.

To mak prymerolle in pasthe tak blanched almondes and flour of prymerose grind it and temper it with swet wyne and good brothe drawinge into the thik mylk put it into a pot with sugur salt and saffron that it haue colour lik prymerolle and boile it that it be stondinge and alay it with flour of rise and serue it as a standinge potage and strawe ther on flour of prymerolle aboue and ye may diaper it with rape rialle in dressinge of some other sewe. [A Noble Boke off Cookry (England, 1468)]

There is also a recipe for primrose in *Two Fifteenth-Century Cookery-Books* that is clearly related.

Cviij - Prymerose. Take other half-pound of Flowre of Rys, .iij. pound of Almaundys, half an vnce of hony and Safroune, and take the flowres of the Prymerose, and grynd hem, and temper hem vppe with Mylke of the Almaundys, and do pouder Gyngere ther-on: boyle it, and plante thin skluce with Rosys, and serue forth. [Two Fifteenth-Century Cookery-Books (England, 1430)]

The description of the dish as "stonding" indicates an extremely thick dish, like very thick oatmeal. The instruction at the end of the *Wagstaff* and *Noble* versions to diaper (decorate all over) with a second recipe appears unique to these two cookbooks. Note that this second dish, Rape Royal, is likely a sweet, thick sauce of raisins and figs.

The name of the recipes suggests a dish to me made around Easter (Pasch), which makes sense given the lack of eggs and the use of flower petals.

130. To Make a Possote

This recipe is a match for recipe 70 from *A Noble Boke off Cookry*.

To mak a posthot, put cow mylk in a pan and set it on the fyer and when it is at boiling do ther in other wyne or ale and no salt then tak it from the fyer and kele it and assone as the curddes gaddure take up the curddes with a saucer or a ladille and serue it and straw ther on pouder of ginger and ye may tak the sam curdde and lay it on the clothe and presse out the wyne and drawe it through a strener with swet wyne put ther to pouder of guinger and sugur and mele it to gedure and serue it as a stonding sewe for sopers and straw ther on anise in comfettes. [A Noble Boke off Cookry (England, 1468)]

One of the minor but interesting differences is that the *Wagstaff* version has "presse out the whey" where the *Noble* version has "presse out the wyne".

131. Pyes of Pares

This recipe is a match for recipe 72 from *A Noble Boke off Cookry*.

To mak pyes of pairis tak and smyt fair buttes of pork and buttes of vele and put it to gedure in a pot with freshe brothe and put ther to a quantite of wyne and boile it tille it be enoughe then put it in to a treene vesselle and put ther to raw yolks of eggs pouder of guinger sugur salt and mynced dates and raissins of corans and mak a good thyn paiste and mak coffyns and put it ther in and bak it welle and serue it. [A Noble Boke off Cookry (England, 1468)]

As with the recipe for Possote, there is an interesting word substitution. The word "clene" (clean) in the *Wagstaff* version is given as "treene" (tree-en, i.e. wooden).

There is also a version of this recipe in *Two Fifteenth-Century Cookery-Books*.

Pies of Parys. Take and smyte faire buttes of porke and buttes of vele togidre, and put hit in a faire potte, And putte thereto faire broth, And a quantite of Wyne, And lete all boile togidre til hit be ynogh; And then take hit fro the fire, and lete kele a litel, and cast ther-to raw yolkes of eyren, and pouudre of gyngeuere, sugre and salt, and mynced dates, reysyns of corence: make then coffyns of feyre past, and do it ther-ynne, and keuere it and lete bake y-nogh. [Two Fifteenth-Century Cookery-Books (England, 1430)]

132. Brinddy

This recipe is a match for recipe 71 from *A Noble Boke off Cookry*.

To mak Breney, put wyne in a pot and clarified hony saunders canelle peper clowes maces pynes dates mynced raissins of corans put ther to vinegar and sett it on the fyer. and let it boile then sethe fegges in wyne grind them and draw them through a strener and cast ther to and let them boile to gedur then tak flour saffron sugur and faire water and mak ther of faire cakes and let them be thyne then cut them bigge lassengis wise and fry them in oile a stonding sewe for sopers and strawe ther on annes in comfets and serue it. [A Noble Boke off Cookry (England, 1468)]

There are also two versions of this recipe in *Two Fifteenth-Century Cookery-Books*.

Prenade. Take wyn, and put hit in a potte, and clarefied honey, sawndres, pouder of peper, Canel, Clowes, Maces, Saffron, pynes, myced dates, and reysons, And cast thereto a litul vinegre, and sette hit ouer the fire, and lete hit boyle; and seth figges in wyn and grynde hem, and draw hem thorgh a streynour, and cast thereto, and let boile al togidre. And then take floure, saffron, sugur, and faire water, and make faire kakes, and late hem be thyn ynogh; And then kutte hem like losinges; And then caste hem in faire oyle, and fry hem a litul while; And then take hem vp oute of the pan, and caste hem to the wessell with the sirippe, altogidre, in a dissh; And therefore thi sirripe most be rennyng ynow, and no3t to stiff; and so serue it forth fore a good potage, in faire disshes all hote. [Two Fifteenth-Century Cookery-Books (England, 1430)]

Bryndons. Take Wyn, and putte in a potte, an clarifiyd hony, an Saunderys, pepir, Safroun, Clowes, Maces, and Quybibys, and mynced Datys, Pynys and Roysonys of Corauns, and a lytil Vynegre, and sethe it on the fyre; an sethe fygys in Wyne, and grynde hem, and draw hem thorw a straynoure, and caste ther-to, an lete hem boyle alle to-gederys; than take fayre flowre, Safroun, Sugre, and Fayre Water, ande make ther-of cakys, and let hem be thinne Inow; than kytte hem y lyke lechyngys,

(Note: long thin strips) an caste hem in fayre Oyle, and fry hem a lytil whyle; thanne take hem owt of the panne, an caste in-to a vesselle with the Syrippe, and so serue hem forth, the bryndonys an the Sirippe, in a dysshe; and let the Sirippe be rennyng, and not to styf. [Two Fifteenth-Century Cookery-Books (England, 1430)]

The name of the *Noble* version, Breny, may be a crude reference to the recipe's appearance. The word "bren" in Middle French could be translated as "excrement."

133. Losyngys opyn
This recipe is a match for recipe 73 from *A Noble Boke off Cookry.*

To mak lossenges fried in lent make a paiste of pured flour knodden with faire water sugur saffron and salt then mak a thyn foile in lossengis the bred of your hond or lese and fry them in oile and serue them iij or iiij in a dysshe. [A Noble Boke off Cookry (England, 1468)]

The difference in titles is a bit unusual. The lack of dairy and eggs clearly marks this as a Lenten recipe, so the title of the *Noble* version isn't exceptional. However there is noting in the recipe that suggests "open" rather than "closed."

134. Harbelet opyn
This recipe is a match for recipe 74 from *A Noble Boke off Cookry.*

To mak hairblad opyne tak Buttes of pork and smyt them to peces boille them in faire water till they be enough do it on a bord and put away the skyne and the bones and hewe it small and put it in a fair bolle then tak parsly ysope and saige and hewe it smale and put it in a bolle do ther to fat of the brothe and boile them and put ther to the fleshe mynced dates clowes mace raissins of corans saffron salt pouder of guinger yolks of eggs and draw them throughe a strener and labour it to gedure welle and mak round coffins and hardyn them in an oven then tak them up and fill them with a dysshe with the stuf and set them in the ovene all opyne and let them bak and serue them. [A Noble Boke off Cookry (England, 1468)]

There are also two recipes from *Two Fifteenth-Century Cookery-Books* that are very similar.

xxxj - Herbelade. Take Buttes of Porke, and smyte hem in pecys, and sette it ouer the fyre; and sethe hem in fayre Watere; and whan it is y-sothe y-now, ley it on a fayre bord, and pyke owt alle the bonys, and hew it smal, and put it in a fayre bolle; than take ysope, Sawge, Percely a gode quantite, and hew it smal, and putte it on a fayre vesselle; than take a lytel of the brothe, that the porke was sothin in, and draw thorw a straynoure, and caste to the Erbys, and 3if it a boyle; thenne take owt the Erbys with a Skymoure fro the brothe, and caste hem to the Porke in the bolle; than mynce Datys smal, and caste hem ther-to, and Roysonys of Coraunce, and Pyne3, and drawe thorw a straynoure 3olkys of Eyroun ther-to, and Sugre, and pouder Gyngere, and Salt, and coloure it a lytel with Safroune; and toyle yt with thin hond al thes to-gederys; than make fayre round cofyns, and harde hem a lytel in the ovyn; than take hem owt, and wyth a dyssche in thin hond, fylle hem fulle of the Stuffe; than sette hem ther-in a-3en; and lat hem bake y-now, and serue forth. [Two Fifteenth-Century Cookery-Books (England, 1430)]

Herbe-blade. Take buttes of Porke, and smyte hem in peces, and sette hit on the fire, and seth it in faire water; And whan hit is soden y-nogh, take it oute, and baude hit, and pike oute the bones, and hewe it small, and putte hit in a faire boll. And take Isop, Sauge, and parcelly a goode quantite; pike hit, and hewe hit small, And put hit in faire vessellez; And take a litul of the broth that the porke was soden yn, and drawe hit thorgh a streynour, and caste to the erbeblade, and yef hit a boyle; then take oute the herbes with a Skymour fro the broth, And cast hem into the porke in the bolle; And then myce faire dates small, And caste hem there-to, And reysons of coraunce, and pynes; And draw rawe yolkes of egges thorgh a straynour, and caste thereto Sugur, powder of Ginger, salt; colour hit with a litull saffron; And trull hit with thi honde, al this togidur in the bolle; And then make faire rownde cofyns, and put hem in the oven, and hard hem a litull, and take hem oute ayen, and with a dissh in thi honde, fil hem full of the stuffe, and sette hem ayen in the oven al open, And let hem bake ynowe. And thenne serue hit forth. [Two Fifteenth-Century Cookery-Books (England, 1430)]

135. Leche fryed

This recipe is clearly related to recipe 75 from *A Noble Boke off Cookry.*

To mak lesche freey tak and cutt tenches in sshevers and put it in hot skaldinge watur and when it rynnyth and yeldithe to gedure ye may do away the watir clene and and put it to clarified buttur hot a gret dele and hony clarified and toile them to gedur with yolks of eggs then tak brod coffyns with lowe lidds as thyn as ye may dryf them and fill them with the stuf and bak them and serue them. [A Noble Boke off Cookry (England, 1468)]

The most notable difference between the two is that where *Wagstaff* calls for cheese, *Noble* has a type of fish (tench). The use of cheese in the recipe is supported by another version from *Two Fifteenth-Century Cookery-Books.*

Lese fryes. Take nessh chese, and pare it clene, and grinde hit in a morter small, and drawe yolkes and white of egges thorgh a streynour, and cast there-to, and grinde hem togidre; then cast thereto Sugur, butter and salt, and put al togidre in a coffyn of faire paast, And lete bake ynowe, and then serue it forthe. [Two Fifteenth-Century Cookery-Books (England, 1430)]

It is likely that the difference between the *Wagstaff* and Noble versions is a copying error where "neshchese" was taken as "tenches". It is also possible that it is a transcription error on the part of Ms. Napier when transcribed *Noble* back in 1882.

136. Bakyn Mete on Fisch Dayes

This recipe is a match for recipe 76 from *A Noble Boke off Cookry*.

> To mak bak metes on fysshe days tak lamprons and strip them with a cloth till they be clene and boile them in watur salt and venegar and labur hem welle in pouder and salt and lay them in coffins then tak a thyk mylk of almonds and draw it up with faire watir or with the brothe of fisshe put ther to pouder sugur and foilis of padley venegar and salt and set them in the ovene and fill them up ther with and serue them. [A Noble Boke off Cookry (England, 1468)]

While there are many other recipes for baked lampreys, none of them are as short and simple as these.

137. A Bakyn Mete Opyn

The title of this recipe was appended to the body of the previous one in the manuscript, which makes it easy to miss.

This is an odd little recipe with no close match in contemporary cookbooks.

138. A Colde Bakyn Mete

I could not find any recipes similar to this one. What's more, the detailed instructions for using gold leaf are unique among the cookbooks I've worked with.

139. Caudell of Almondys

Caudle recipes are fairly common in medieval cookbooks, including two in *A Noble Boke off Cookry*, but none are a close match for this version.

> To mak cawdelle dalmond tak unblanched almondes and bray them and draw them with wyne put ther to pouder of guinger and sugur and boile all to gedur and colore it with saffron and salt it and serue it. [A Noble Boke off Cookry (England, 1468)]

To mak a cawdelle of almondes tak blanched almondes and draw them up with wyne put ther to saffron and salt and serue it. [A Noble Boke off Cookry (England, 1468)]

Cawdelle de Almaunde. Take Raw Almaundys, and grynde hem, an temper hem vp with gode ale, and a lytil Water, and draw it thorw a straynoure in-to a fayre potte, and late it boyle a whyle: and caste ther-to Safroun, Sugre, and Salt, and than serue it forth al hotte in maner of potage. [Two Fifteenth-Century Cookery-Books (England, 1430)]

Caudell de Almondes. Take rawe almondes, and grinde hem, And temper hem with goode ale and a litul water; and drawe hem thorgh a streynour into a faire potte, and lete hit boyle awhile; And cast there-to saffron, Sugur and salt, and serue hit forth hote. [Two Fifteenth-Century Cookery-Books (England, 1430)]

140. For to sle aner of foules & roste hem & serve hem forth
This recipe is a match for recipe 77 from *A Noble Boke off Cookry*.

To sley a swan and allmaner of fowle and to dight them, tak a swan and cutt him in the roof of the mouthe toward the brayne of the hed and lett hym bled to dethe then kep the blod to colour the chaudron and knyt the nek and let him dye then skald hym drawe hym rost him and serue hym with chaudron. [A Noble Boke off Cookry (England, 1468)]

While the title of the *Wagstaff* version was clearly copied in error, I find it interesting that the *Wagstaff* recipe correctly separates the methods of killing the swan with an "or" where the *Noble* version has "and".

141. Crane Rostyd
This recipe is a match for recipe 81 from *A Noble Boke off Cookry*.

A crayne let him bled as a swann and draw hym at the vent then fold up his leggs and cut off his wings by the joint next to the body then wind the nek about the broche and put the bill in the brest against the wings and leggs as he gothe, and ye sauce hym tak and anynte hym and sauce hym with pouder of guinger mustard venygar and salt and serue it, also ye may sauce it with sauce pelito. [A Noble Boke off Cookry (England, 1468)]

One odd difference between the two is that *Wagstaff* instructs the reader to mince the crane before saucing it. That instruction is echoed in two other versions of the recipe from *Two Fifteenth-Century Cookery-Books*.

Crane roste. Capitulum c.vij. Take a crane, and cutt hym in the rofe of the mouth, and lete him blede to deth: and cast a-wey the blode, and schalde hym, and draw hym vndyr the wynge or att the vent, and folde vpp hys legges att the kneys vndir the thye; and cutt of the wyngys next iunte the body, and lete hym haue hys heuede and hys necke on; saue take awey the wesyng, and wynde the necke a-boute the spyte, and bynde hit, and putt the bille in the body and the golett; and reyse the wynges and the legges as of a gose; and yiff thou schalt sauce hym, mynce hym fyrst, and sauce hym withe pouudre of pepyr, and gyngeuere and mustarde, vynegre and salt, and serue hym forth. [Two Fifteenth-Century Cookery-Books (England, 1430)]

Crane rosted. Lete a Crane blode in the mouthe as thou diddist a Swan; fold vp his legges, kutte of his winges at the ioynte next the body, drawe him, Wynde the nekke abought the spit; putte the bill in his brest: his sauce is to be mynced with pouder of ginger, vynegre, and Mustard. [Two Fifteenth-Century Cookery-Books (England, 1430)]

The last word of the *Wagstaff* and *Noble* versions, "sylito/pelito", is possibly a reference to pellitory (*Anacyclus pyrethrum*).

142. Fesaunte Rostyd
This recipe is a match for recipe 78 from *A Noble Boke off Cookry*.

A fessand let him blod in the mouth to the dethe then pull him dry and cut of the hed and the nek and the leggs from the body par boile hym and lard him then put the kneys in the vent and raft hym and raise his leggs and his wings as it were a henne and no sauce but salt. [A Noble Boke off Cookry (England, 1468)]

There are also two clearly related recipes in *Two Fifteenth-Century Cookery-Books*.

Fesaunt rost. Capitulum cviij. Lete a fesaunt blode in the mouth, and lete hym blede to deth; and pulle hym, and draw hym, and kutt a-wey the necke by the body, and the legges by the kne, and perbuille hym, and larde hym, and putt the knese in the vent: and rost hym, and reise hym vpp, hys legges and hys wynges, as off an henne; and no sauce butt salt. [Two Fifteenth-Century Cookery-Books (England, 1430)]

ffesaunte rosted. Lete a ffesaunte blode in the mouthe as a crane, And lete him blede to dethe; pull him dry, kutte awey his hede and the necke by the body, and the legges by the kne, and putte the kneys in at the vente, and roste him: his sauce is Sugur and mustard. [Two Fifteenth-Century Cookery-Books (England, 1430)]

This last recipe is especially interesting in that it specifies seasoning the phesant with something other than salt.

143. Pertrich Rostyd
This recipe is a match for recipe 79 from *A Noble Boke off Cookry*.

A pertuehe tak a fedir and put it in to his hed and let hym dye and pulle hym dry and drawe hym and rost hym as ye wold raise the legges and wingys of an henne and mynee hym sauce hym with wyne pouder of guinger and salt and warme it on the fyere and serue it. [A Noble Boke off Cookry (England, 1468)]

The *Noble* version makes it clear that the feather is used in killing the partridge.

As with the recipe for roast pheasant, there is a related recipe in *Two Fifteenth-Century Cookery-Books*, again with significant differences in the spicing.

> Partrich rosted. Take a partrich, and sle him in the nape of the hede with a fethur; dight him, larde him, and roste him as thou doest a ffesaunte in the same wise, And serue him forth; then sauce him with wyne, pouder of ginger and salt, And sette hit in a dissh on the fuyre til hit boyle; then cast powder ginger, Canell, thereon, And kutte him so; or elles ete him with sugur and Mustard. [Two Fifteenth-Century Cookery-Books (England, 1430)]

144. Quayle Rostyd
This recipe is a match for recipe 80 from *A Noble Boke off Cookry*.

> A quayle tak and sley hym and rost hym as a pertuehe and raise his legges and his wyngs as a hene and no sauce but salt and serue it. [A Noble Boke off Cookry (England, 1468)]

There is a corresponding recipe in *Two Fifteenth-Century Cookery-Books*, but it calls for cameline sauce rather than just salt.

> Quayle rosted. Take a Quayle, and sle him, And serue him as thou doest a partrich in all Degre. His Sauce is sauce gamelyne. [Two Fifteenth-Century Cookery-Books (England, 1430)]

145. Heyron Rostyd
This recipe is a match for recipe 82 from *A Noble Boke off Cookry*.

> A heron let hym bled in the mouthe as a crayne skald hym and draw hym at the vent and cut away the bone of the nek and let the hed be on stille with the skyne of the nek and folde the nek about the broche and put the hed in at the gollet as a crayne and brek away the bone from the kne to the foot and let the skyn be hole and cut the wings at the joint next the body then put hym on a broche and bynde the leggs to the spit with the skyn of the leggs and rost hym and raise his leggs and his wings

as a crayne and sauce him with vinegar mustard poudered guinger and salt and serue it. [A Noble Boke off Cookry (England, 1468)]

Aside from having some of the instructions in a different order, where the *Noble* version has "from the knee to the foot" the *Wagstaff* version has "from the neck to the font". I believe the *Noble* version is correct in this case. It is also odd that both versions appear to have the wings cut off but then go on to "raise the wings" for presentation.

There are also two versions of this recipe in *Two Fifteenth-Century Cookery-Books*.

> Heron rost. Capitulum c.x. Take an heron, and lete hym blode in the mouth as an crane, and scalde hym and draw hym att the vent as a crane; and cutt awey the boon of the necke, and folde the necke a-boute the spite, and putt the hede ynne att the golet as a crane; and breke awey the boon fro the kne to the fote, and lete the skyn be stille, and cutt the wyng att the Joynte next the body, and putt hem on a spite: and bynde hys legges to the spyte with the skynne of the legges, and lete rost, and reyse the legges and the wynges as of a crane, and sauce hym with vynegre, and mustard, and pouudre of gyngeuere, and sett hym forth. [Two Fifteenth-Century Cookery-Books (England, 1430)]

> Heron rosted. Take a Heron; lete him blode as a crane, And serue him in al poyntes as a crane, in scalding, drawing, and kuttyng the bone of the nekke a-wey, And lete the skyn be on, and roste him and sause him as the Crane; breke awey the bone fro the kne to the fote, And lete the skyn be on. [Two Fifteenth-Century Cookery-Books (England, 1430)]

146. Bytare Rostyd

This recipe is a close match for recipe 83 in *A Noble Boke off Cookry*.

> A Bittur take and sley him in the mouthe as a heron drawe him as a henne and fold up his leggs as a crayne and lett the wings be on then tak a waye the bone of the nek as ye did a heron

and put the hed into the gullet or in to the shulder then raise hym and raise his leggs and his wynges as a herone and no sauce but salt. [A Noble Boke off Cookry (England, 1468)]

There are also two versions of this recipe in *Two Fifteenth-Century Cookery-Books*.

Bitore roste. Capitulum cxj. Slee a bytour in the mouth as an heron, and draw hym as an henne, and fold vppe hys legges as a crane; and lete the wynges be on, and take the boon of the necke all awey as of an heron: and putt the hedde in the golet or in the shuldre, and rost hym; and ryse the legges and the wynges as thou dost of an heron, and no sauce butt salt: and sett hym forth. [Two Fifteenth-Century Cookery-Books (England, 1430)]

Bytor rosted. Take a Bitour, sle him in the mouthe, skalde him, serue him in all poyntes as thou doest a Crane, but lete him haue on his winges when he is rosted, And serue him forthe. [Two Fifteenth-Century Cookery-Books (England, 1430)]

147. Egrett Rostyd
This recipe is a close match for recipe 84 in *A Noble Boke off Cookry*.

An Egret tak and brek his nek and cutt of the roof of his mouthe and scald him and draw him as a henne then cutt of his wings by the body and fold up his legs as a bittur and rost hym and raise his leggs and his wings as a heron and no sauce but salt. [A Noble Boke off Cookry (England, 1468)]

There are also two versions of this recipe in *Two Fifteenth-Century Cookery-Books*.

Egrett rost. Capitulum cxij. Breke an egrettes nekke, or cut the rofe of hys mouth, as of a crane, and scalde hym, and draw hym as an henne; and cutt of hys wynges by the body, and the heued and the necke by the body, and folde hys legges as a bitore, and rost hym: and no sauce butt salt. [Two Fifteenth-Century Cookery-Books (England, 1430)]

Egrete rosted. Take an Egrete, sle him as a Crane, skalde him and drawe him, and kutte his winges, and folde his legges as a crane, and roste him, And serue him forth; and no sauce but salte. [Two Fifteenth-Century Cookery-Books (England, 1430)]

148. Curlew Rostyd

This recipe is a match for recipe 85 from *A Noble Boke off Cookry*.

A Curlew tak and sley him in the mouthe as a fessand pull hym dry cutt of his wings and draw hym as a henne and fold up his feet like an egret and let his hed and his nek be one and tak away the nether lipe and the throt holle and put his bille in his shuldurs and rost hym and raise his leggs and his wings as a henne and no sauce but salt. [A Noble Boke off Cookry (England, 1468)]

There is another version of this recipe in *Two Fifteenth-Century Cookery-Books*.

Curlewe rosted. Take a Curlewe, sle him as a Crane, pul him dry, kutte of the winges by the body, drawe him, dight him as a Henne, And folde vp his legges as a crane; lete his necke and his hede be on; take awey the nether lippe and throte boll, and put his hede in at his shuldur, and roste him as a Crane, and no sauuce but salte. [Two Fifteenth-Century Cookery-Books (England, 1430)]

149. Grew Rostyd

This recipe is a match for recipe 86 from *A Noble Boke off Cookry*.

A Brewe sley him in the mouthe as a curlewe skald hym and drawe hym as an henne then brek his leggs at the kne and tak away the bone from the kne to the foot as a heron cut of the nek by the bodye then rost hym and raise his winges and his legges as a heron and no sauce but salt. [A Noble Boke off Cookry (England, 1468)]

There is another version of this recipe in *Two Fifteenth-Century Cookery-Books*.

> Brewe rosted. Take a Brewe, sle him as the Curlewe, skalde him, drawe him as a hen, breke his legges at the kne, and take awey the bone fro the kne to the fote, as a heron; And kutte the winges by the body, and his hede by the body, and put him on a spitte, And bynde his legges as a heron; roste him, reyse his legges and his winges as a heron, And take no maner sauce butte salte. [Two Fifteenth-Century Cookery-Books (England, 1430)]

It is interesting that the mistranscription "brew" for grue occurs in both *Noble* and *Two Fifteenth-Century Cookery-Books*.

150. Conynggys Rostyd
This recipe is a match for recipe 87 from *A Noble Boke off Cookry*.

> A conye tak and drawe hym and parboile hym rost hym and lard hym then raise his leggs and hys winges and sauce hym with venegar and pouder of guinger and serue it. [A Noble Boke off Cookry (England, 1468)]

There is also a related recipe in *Two Fifteenth-Century Cookery-Books*.

> Conyng. Take a Conyng, fle him, And draw him aboue and byneth, And parboile him, And larde him, and roste him, And late the hede be on; And vndo him, and sauce him with sauce, ginger, And vergeous, and powder of ginger, And thenne serue hit forth. [Two Fifteenth-Century Cookery-Books (England, 1430)]

There are a couple of oddities here. The first is the doubling up on ginger in the *Noble* and Two Fifteenth-Century recipes. The *Noble* version doesn't do this, but has replaced the verjuice with vinegar.

The second, and more amusing, oddity is the reference in *Noble* to the coney's wings.

151. Rabets Rostyd

This recipe is a match for recipe 88 from *A Noble Boke off Cookry*.

> To rost rabettes tak and flay them drawe them and rost them
> and let their heddes be on first parboile them as a cony or ye
> rost them and serue them. [A Noble Boke off Cookry
> (England, 1468)]

There is also a related recipe in *Two Fifteenth-Century Cookery-Books*.

> Rabette rosted. Take a Rabette, and sle him, And drawe him,
> And lete his hede be on, as a Conyng; roste him as a Conyng,
> And serue him forth. [Two Fifteenth-Century Cookery-Books
> (England, 1430)]

The replacement of "slay" with "flay" in the *Noble* version is most
likely a transcription error.

152. Sarcell Rostyd

This recipe is a match for recipe 89 from *A Noble Boke off Cookry*.

> To rost a sarcelle brek his nek and pulle hym dry and drawe
> hym as a chekyn cutt of his feet his wings and his nek and rost
> him and raise his leggs and his wings as a heron and no sauce
> but salt, and serve it. [A Noble Boke off Cookry (England,
> 1468)]

There is also a related recipe in *Two Fifteenth-Century Cookery-Books*.

> Sorcell rosted. Take a Sorcell or a tele, and breke his necke, and
> pul him dry, And draw him as a chekon, and kutte off his fete
> and winges by the body and the nekke, and roste him, and reise
> his winges and his legges as a heron, if he be a Sorcell; And no
> sauce but salt. [Two Fifteenth-Century Cookery-Books
> (England, 1430)]

153. Plover Rostyd

This recipe is a match for recipe 90 from *A Noble Boke off Cookry*.

> To rost a plouer tak and brek his skull and drawe hym as a
> chekyne and cutt of his legges and his wings by the body and
> rost hym and raise his legges and his wings as a henne and no
> sauce but salt and serue it. [A Noble Boke off Cookry
> (England, 1468)]

There are also two related recipes in *Two Fifteenth-Century Cookery-Books*.

> Plouer rost. Capitulum Cxix. Breke the skulle of a plouere, and
> pull hym drye, and draw hym as a chike, and cutte the legges
> and the wynges by the body, and the heued and necke all-so,
> and roste hym, and reyse the legges and wynges as an henne:
> and no sauce butt salt. [Two Fifteenth-Century Cookery-
> Books (England, 1430)]

> Plouer. Take a plouer, and breke his skoll, and pull him dry,
> And drawe him as a chekon, And kutte the legges and the
> winges as a henne; And no sauce but salt. [Two Fifteenth-
> Century Cookery-Books (England, 1430)]

I find the instruction to break the plover's skull a bit unusual. It's
the first step in all of the related recipes, where the method of
slaughter is usually given, so I expect that was the preferred
method for killing them.

154. Snyte Rostyd

This recipe is a match for recipe 91 from *A Noble Boke off Cookry*.

> To rost a snytte tak and slay hym as a plouer and pull him dry
> and let his nek be hole saue the wings and let the hed be on
> and put the hed in the shulder and fold up his legges as ye did
> a crayne and cut of his winges then rost hym and raise his
> winges and his leggs and shulders as a plouer and no sauce but
> salt. [A Noble Boke off Cookry (England, 1468)]

There is also a related recipe in *Two Fifteenth-Century Cookery-Books*.

> Snyte rost. Capitulum Cxx. Slee a snyte as a plouere, and lete hys necke be hole saue the wesyng; and lete hys heuede be on, and putt it in the schuldre, and folde vppe his legges as a crane, and cutt his wynges and roste hym, and reyse hys legges and wynges as an henne; and no sauce butt salt. [Two Fifteenth-Century Cookery-Books (England, 1430)]

155. Woodcok Rostyd

This recipe is a match for recipe 92 from *A Noble Boke off Cookry*.

> To rost a wodcok tak and sley him as a snyet and pulle hym dry or brek his bak but kep his skull hole and drawe hym as a snyt and put his bille through bothe hys sides then rost hym and raise his leggs and his wings as a hen and no sauce but salt. [A Noble Boke off Cookry (England, 1468)]

There is also a related recipe in *Two Fifteenth-Century Cookery-Books*.

> Wodekok. Take a wodecok, and sle him as the plouer; pul him dry, or elles breke his bakke, And lete the sculle be hole; drawe him, And kutte of his winges by the body, and turne vp the legges as thou doest of a crane; put his bill thorgh bothe his thighes; roste him, And reise his legges And his winges, as thou doest of all maner of other clouen fote fowle. [Two Fifteenth-Century Cookery-Books (England, 1430)]

156. Kyd Rostyd

This recipe is a match for recipe 93 from *A Noble Boke off Cookry*.

> To rost a kyd tak and slit of the skyn at the throt and seche for the vanys on bothe sides the gorge and cut them and slit them and put there in bothe the forelegs and the hinder leggs bothe sides eliche and prik them and parboile hem and rost them and lard them and serue them with sauce guinger. [A Noble Boke off Cookry (England, 1468)]

There is also a related recipe in *Two Fifteenth-Century Cookery-Books*.

> Kede rosted. Take a kydde, and slytte the skyn in the throte, And seke the veyne, and kut him, and lete him blede to deth; and fle him, And larde him, And trusse his legges in the sides, and roste him, And reyse the shuldres and legges, and sauce hit with vinegre and salte. [Two Fifteenth-Century Cookery-Books (England, 1430)]

While the instructions in *Two Fifteenth-Century Cookery-Books* seem a bit clearer, I find it interesting that it calls for vinegar and salt instead of ginger sauce.

157. Vele Rostyd

There is a closely related recipe in *Two Fifteenth-Century Cookery-Books*.

> Vele rosted. Take faire brestes of vele, And parboyle hem, And larde hem, And roste hem, And then serue hem forth. [Two Fifteenth-Century Cookery-Books (England, 1430)]

It is odd that, given the long run of 12 duplicated recipes in the same sequence, this short entry was left out of *A Noble Boke off Cookry*.

158. Venyson Rostyd

This recipe is a match for recipe 94 from *A Noble Boke off Cookry*.

> To rost venison tak feletes of venyson bound and cutt away the skyne and parboile it and let it be throughe stiff then lard it with salt and put it on a smale broche and rost it and if it be ned leche it abrod in leskes and lay them in a dysshe and strow on pouder of guinger and salt, and ye may do with buttes of venyson in the same manner. [A Noble Boke off Cookry (England, 1468)]

159. The Syde of a Dere of His Grece

While this is a fairly simple recipe, with instructions that are almost stereotypical for how lean meat was roasted in the fifteenth century, I could not find any matching recipes in other sources.

160. Chikenes Farsyd

There is a related recipe in Ancient Cookery.

> Farsure for chekyns. Take fressh porke, and fethe hit, and hew hit smal, and grinde hit wel; and put therto harde zolkes of egges, and medel hom wel togedur, and do therto raifynges of corance, and pouder of cancl, and maces, and quibibz (cubebs), and of clowes al hole; and colour hit with saffron, and do hit into the chekyns; and then parboyle hom, and roste, and endore (baste) hom with rawc zolkes of egges, and fiaume hom if hit be nede, and serve hit forthe. [Ancient Cookery, (England, 1425)]

The *Wagstaff* recipe seems slightly confused, so this might be a combination of two or more recipes. The use of the word "plunge" ("blonge") instead of parboil is a bit strange.

161. Chikenes Endoryd

This recipe is a match for recipe 96 from *A Noble Boke off Cookry*.

> To mak chekyns endort tak chekyns and skald them and tak out the brest bone and saue the skyn hole then rost them till they be enoughe and endore them with yolkes of eggs and when the endoringe is stiff let them rost no more also ye may rost kidde and endore them in the same manner. [A Noble Boke off Cookry (England, 1468)]

There is also another version in *Two Fifteenth-Century Cookery-Books*

> Chike endored. Take a chike, and drawe him, and roste him, And lete the fete be on, and take awey the hede; then make batur of yolkes of eyron and floure, and caste there-to pouder of ginger, and peper, saffron and salt, and pouder hit faire til

163

hit be rosted ynogh. [Two Fifteenth-Century Cookery-Books (England, 1430)]

The instructions in *Wagstaff* and Noble for removing the breast bone and saving the skin are unusual. I suppose removing the skin might help the batter stick, but why save the skin whole and why remove the breast bone?

162. Fylets of Porke Endoryd
This recipe is a match for recipe 97 from *A Noble Boke off Cookry.*

> To dight felettes of pork tak and rost felettes of pork and endor them with the same bater ye did the chekins and rost them and serue them. [A Noble Boke off Cookry (England, 1468)]

That being said, the instructions from the *Wagstaff* version are actually much closer to those in the following recipe from *Two Fifteenth-Century Cookery-Books.*

> ffelettes of Porke endored. Take ffelettes of porke, and roste hem faire, And endore hem with the same batur as thou doest a cheke as he turneth aboute the spitte, And serue him forth. [Two Fifteenth-Century Cookery-Books (England, 1430)]

163. Capons of Hyee Grece Rostyd
This recipe is a match for recipe 98 from *A Noble Boke off Cookry.*

> To rost capon or gose tak and drawe his leuer and his guttes at the vent and his grece at the gorge and tak the leef of grece parsly ysope rosmarye and ij lengs of saige and put to the grece and hew it smale and hew yolks of eggs cromed raissins of corans good poudurs saffron and salt melled to gedure and fers the capon there withe and broche hym and let hym be stanche at the vent and at the gorge that the stuffur go not out and rost hym long with a soking fyere and kep the grece that fallithe to baist hym and kepe hym moist till ye serue hym and sauce hym

with wyne and guingere as capons be. [A Noble Boke off Cookry (England, 1468)]

The *Wagstaff* version is missing a few words, along with the option of cooking goose, and seems to be a bit confused.

164. Capon Stewed
This recipe is related to recipe 103 from *A Noble Boke off Cookry*.

To stew a capon tak parsly saige ysope rosmary and brek them between your handes and stop the capon ther with and colour it with saffron and couch it in an erthen pot and lay splentes under nethe and about the sides of the pot and straw erbes about the capon and put ther to a quart of wyn and non other licour then couer the pot close that no brothe passe out then set it on a charcole fyere and stew it softly and when it is enoughe set it on a wispe of strawe that it touche not the ground for brekinge then tak out the capon with a prik and luk yf it be enoughe or els stewe it better and mak a ceripe of good wyne mynced dates and canelle anld draw it with the same wyne put ther to raissins of corands sugur saffron and salt and guinger and wyn then lay the capon in a dysshe and put the fat of the sew to the ceripe and poure it on the capon and serue it. [A Noble Boke off Cookry (England, 1468)]

There is also a related recipe in *Two Fifteenth-Century Cookery-Books* that similar to the *Noble* version.

Capons Stwed. Take parcelly, Sauge, Isoppe, Rose Mary, and tyme, and breke hit bitwen thi hondes, and stoppe the Capon there-with; colour hym with Safferon, and couche him in a erthen potte, or of brasse, and ley splentes vnderneth and al abou3t the sides, that the Capon touche no thinge of the potte; strawe good herbes in the potte, and put there-to a pottel of the best wyn that thou may gete, and none other licour; hele the potte with a close led, and stoppe hit abou3te with dogh or bater, that no eier come oute; And set hit on the faire charcole, and lete it seeth easly and longe till hit be ynowe. And if hit be an erthen potte, then set hit on the fire whan thou takest hit downe, and lete hit not touche the grounde for breking; And whan the hete is ouer past, take oute the Capon with a prik; then make a sirippe of wyne, Reysons of corance, sugur and safferon, And boile hit a litull; medel pouder of Ginger with a litul of the same wyn, and do thereto; then do awey the fatte of the sewe of the Capon, And do the Siryppe to the sewe, and powre hit on the capon, and serue it forth. [Two Fifteenth-Century Cookery-Books (England, 1430)]

Neither of these recipes has the section in the middle of the *Wagstaff* version, though there is a recipe in MS Pepys 1047 that seems to be closer.

Capons stewed. Take percelly Isope sage Rosemary And tyme breke hit betwene thy hands and stoppe thy capons ther with and color them with saferon And put them yn A erthyn pot or els in brasse for erth is better. And lay splentys underneth and all a boute the sydes so that the capons tuche not the sydes nother the bottom and cast of the same herbys in to þe pot A mong the capons And put a quart or A pynte of the best wyne that thow cansye gette and no other licour And set A lydde ther A pon that wyll ly with yn the brym. And make batur of white of eggys & floure And put betwene the brym A paper lefe or els lyncloth that the batur may stop hit sowrely þat no eyre com owte loke þat hit be thyke of bature And set thy pot on A charecole fyre to the myd syde & se þat the lydde ryse not with the hette and let hit stew esely and long and whan þow supposyth hit is enowgh take hit fro the fyre yf hit be A pot of erth set hit upon a wyspe of ftraw that hit toche not the cold grownde And when the hete is well drawn and over past take of the lydde And take owte thy capons with a stycke And ley them in A noþer vessell and make A syrryp of Wyne And mynct datys and Cannell drawn with the same wyne do ther to rasyns of corance sugur safferon And salt boyle hit A litill And cast yn powder of gynger with a litell of the same wyne do the sew to the syrryppe a boue upon the capons And serue hem furth with A rybbe of beffe ever more a capon on a dysche. [MS Pepys 1047 (England, ca. 1500)]

165. Petydawe
This recipe is a match for recipe 99 from *A Noble Boke off Cookry*.

> To mak apetito tak the garbage of yonge gees heddes nekes wings feet gessern hert and the lever and boille them welle then lay them on a bord and cut the wings the feet and the gesserns the hert the leuer and the lungs and fry them in fair grece then tak pouder of pepper salt and yolks of eggs draw throughe a strener and put them into the frying pan when it is hardenyd turn it and fry it not to myche but that it may hold ethe to gedure and serue it. [A Noble Boke off Cookry (England, 1468)]

The name of the recipe (petydawe/apetito) is a bit cryptic, but it appears to be related to two French recipes called "small feet" (petits pieds).

> Small feet, livers and gizzards [of geese]. Cook them very well in wine and water, and put them on a plate with some parsley and vinegar on top. [Le Viandier de Taillevent (France, ca. 1380)]

> SMALL FEET. Take gizzards and livers and put to cook in wine and water, first the gizzards and last the livers, then put in a dish with minced parsley and vinegar. [Le Menagier de Paris (France, 1393)]

166. Goose or Capons Farsyd
There is a recipe for stuffed goose or capon, number 100, in *A Noble Boke off Cookry*, but it isn't a very good match.

> To fasse goos or capon tak parsly saige and isope suet and parboile it in freche brothe then tak it up and put ther to herd yolks of eggs hewene then tak grapes mynced onyons and pouder of ginger canelle peppur and salt and fers the goos or capon with it and rost them and serue them. [A Noble Boke off Cookry (England, 1468)]

The version in *Two Fifteenth-Century Cookery-Books* is much closer to the *Wagstaff* version.

> Goce or Capon farced. Take parcill, Swynes grece, or suet of shepe, and parboyle hem in faire water and fressh boyling broth; And then take yolkes of eyeron hard y-sodde, and hew hem smale, with the herbes and the salte; and caste thereto pouder of Ginger, Peper, Canell, and salte, and Grapes in tyme of yere; And in other tyme, take oynons, and boile hem; and whan they ben yboiled ynowe with the herbes and with the suet, al thes togidre, then put all in the goos, or in the Capon; And then late him roste ynogh. [Two Fifteenth-Century Cookery-Books (England, 1430)]

167. Pygges Yfarsyd

This recipe is a match for recipe 101 from *A Noble Boke off Cookry*.

> To mak a pigge harsed tak freche pork sodene tender and do away the skyne and the bones then hew the flesshe and half a dossen figges there with and grind them with yolks of eggs and put ther to raissins poudur sugur saffron and salt fat pork and grated bred and cows creme and fars the pige and sow it and rost it and serue it with sauce guinger. [A Noble Boke off Cookry (England, 1468)]

Note that the phrase "with ale" in the *Wagstaff* version probably means "withall" (therewith) rather than to "along with ale".

168. Brestys of Motyn yn Sauce

This recipe is a match for recipe 102 from *A Noble Boke off Cookry*.

> To mak Brestis of moton in sauce tak brestes of moton rost them and chope them then chauf vergious on the fiere put ther to pouder venyger and salt and cast on thy moton and serue it. [A Noble Boke off Cookry (England, 1468)]

There is also a version in *Two Fifteenth-Century Cookery-Books*.

Take faire brestes of Mutton rosted, and chopp hem; And then take Vergeous, and chaaf hit in a Vessell ouer the fire, and caste there-to powder ginger; and then caste the chopped brest in a dissh, And caste the sauce al hote there-on, And serue hit forth.   [Two Fifteenth-Century Cookery-Books (England, 1430)]

169. Dyghtyng of All Maner of Fisch Trought Boyled
This recipe is a match for recipe 104 from *A Noble Boke off Cookry*.

To boill a trout tak and nawpe hym in the hed and mak a sauce of faire water and salt and parsly and when it begynnythe to boile strene it then drawe hym at the belly and ye will haue hym rond cutt hym in the backe in ij or iij places and drawe hym iij stoches by the hed then sethe hym and serue hym furthe with vert sauce cold and foilis of parsly, or els sethe the pouche as ye do of a pik and mynce it with the grave and do that to pouder of guinger and serue it.   [A Noble Boke off Cookry (England, 1468)]

There is also a version in *Two Fifteenth-Century Cookery-Books*.

Troute boyled. Take a troute, and nape him; And make faire sauce of water, parcely, and salt, and whan hit bigynneth to boile, skeme hit clene; and drawe him in the bely; and if thou wilt haue him rounde, kut him in the bakke in two or thre places, but no3t thorgh, And drawe him in the sket (Note: Douce MS. skoch) next the hede, as thou doest a rounde pike; and the sauce is verge sauce; or elles seth the pouche as the dost the pouche of a pike, and myce hem with the grauey, and pouder of ginger; and serue him forth colde, and cast the foiles of parcelly, y-wet in vinegre, on him in a dissh.   [Two Fifteenth-Century Cookery-Books (England, 1430)]

The title of the *Wagstaff* version appears to be a concatenation of a section heading ("Dyghtyng of All Maner of Fisch") and the recipe name ("Trought Boyled"), though in the manuscript it is all on one line with no separator between the two and with the whole line being underlined in red.

170. Crab or Lopstere

This recipe is a match for recipe 105 from *A Noble Boke off Cookry.*

> To dight crabe or lopster tak crabe or lopster and stop hym at the vent with one of the litille clees and sethe hym in clene water or els stop hym in the same manner and cast hym in an ovene and let hym bak and serue it with venygar. [A Noble Boke off Cookry (England, 1468)]

There is also a version in *Two Fifteenth-Century Cookery-Books.* HARLEIAN MS. 4016, ab. 1450 A.D.

> Crabbe or Lopster boiled. Take a crabbe or a lopster, and stop him in the vente with on of hire clees, and seth him in water, and no salt; or elles stoppe him in the same maner, and cast him in an oven, and bake him, and serue him forth colde. And his sauce is vinegre. [Two Fifteenth-Century Cookery-Books (England, 1430)]

The *Wagstaff* version is made confusing by the omission of the word "claw". Oddly, the *Noble* version is the only one that doesn't say to serve the crab cold.

171. Breme yn Sauce

This recipe is a match for recipe 106 from *A Noble Boke off Cookry.*

> To dight a breme in sauce tak and stale hym and drawe hym at the belly and prik hym at the chyne and broylle him on a gredyrne till he be enoughe then tak wyne boiled and cast it to pouder of guinger and vergius then lay the breme in a dysshe and poure on the ceripe and serue it. [A Noble Boke off Cookry (England, 1468)]

There is another version in *Two Fifteenth-Century Cookery-Books.* HARLEIAN MS. 4016, ab. 1450 A.D.

> Breme rost ensauce. Take a breme, and scald him, (but no3t to moche,) and drawe him in the bely, and pryk him thorgh the chyne bon ij. or iij. (Note: twies or thries) with a knyfe, and

roste him on a gredire. And take wyne, and boile hit, and cast there-to pouder ginger, vergeous, and salt, and cast on the breme in a dissh, and serue him forth hote. [Two Fifteenth-Century Cookery-Books (England, 1430)]

172. Breme yn Brace
This recipe is a match for recipe 107 from *A Noble Boke off Cookry*.

To dight a breme in brasse ye shall dight hym in the same manner then tak pouder of canelle and draw theme throughe a strener with red wyn put ther to hole clowes maces pynes and sanders then set it on the fyere and when yt is boilling put ther to pouder of guinger venygar or vergius and let it be chargaut of pouders and lay the breme on a dysshe and pour on the brase and serue it. [A Noble Boke off Cookry (England, 1468)]

173. Tench yn Brace
This recipe is a match for recipe 108 from *A Noble Boke off Cookry*.

To dight a tenche in brasse splat hym by the bak through the hed let the belly be hole do away the draught and stoche hym a litille outwhart on the fische sid and lay them on a gredirn till they be enoughe then lay it in a disshe the fische sid upward and tak the same brase ye tok to the breme and pour ther on and serue it. [A Noble Boke off Cookry (England, 1468)]

There is another, more detailed version in *Two Fifteenth-Century Cookery-Books*. HARLEIAN MS. 4016, ab. 1450 A.D.

Tenche in brase. Take a tenche, and nape him, and slyt him in the bak thorgh the hede and taile, And drawe him; and then make sauce of water and salt. And whan hit bigynneth to boyle, skeme it clene, and cast the tenche therein, and seth him; And take him vppe, and pul of the skyn, And ley him flatte, and the bely vpwardes in a dissh. And then take percelly and oynons And hewe hem small to-giders; And cast there-to pouder of Ginger, and cast hit in vinegre; And caste all on the tenche in the dissh, and serue him forthe colde. [Two Fifteenth-Century Cookery-Books (England, 1430)]

174. Sole yn Brace
This recipe is a match for recipe 109 from *A Noble Boke off Cookry*.

> To mak a sole in brasse tak and sley soiles and draw hym and rost hym and lay hym in a dysshe and mak the same bras ye did to the breme saue clowes and maces and serue it. [A Noble Boke off Cookry (England, 1468)]

The phrase "poudyr hit on" in the *Wagstaff* version may be a copying error for "pour it on".

175. Storgeon
This recipe is a match for recipe 110 from *A Noble Boke off Cookry*.

> To boile sturgion tak and cutt of the fynnys from the taile to the hed and chyne hym as a samon and cutt his fides in faire peces and mak a sauce of water and salt and when it boileth scom it clene and cast in the peces and let them boile and serve them. [A Noble Boke off Cookry (England, 1468)]

There is another, more detailed version in *Two Fifteenth-Century Cookery-Books*. HARLEIAN MS. 4016, ab. 1450 A.D.

> Take a Sturgeon, and kut of the vyn fro the tayle to the hede, on the bakke; and chyne him and boyle him. And whan hit boileth, skeme it, and caste parcelly there-to, And lete hem boyle ynowe, And then take him vppe, And serue him forth colde with leves of parcelly wet in vinegre, and caste there-on in the dissh; And sauce ther-to is vinegre. [Two Fifteenth-Century Cookery-Books (England, 1430)]

It is notable that both the *Wagstaff* and *Two Fifteenth-Century* versions use "vyn" in place of fin.

176. Haddok yn Cyve
This recipe is a match for recipe 111 from *A Noble Boke off Cookry*.

To dight haddok in covy drawe haddok at the belly and he be
large cut of the hed and rost the body on a gredirne till he be
enoughe then stewe bred in the brothe of samon or other good
fisshe draw liere with the brothe hew parsly put it to red wyn
hole clowes maces pouder of pepper and a gooddele of
canella then tak the lever and the pouche of an haddok and
hew it and put it in a possuet and raissins of corans saffron
sanders and salt and boile it and sesson it with pouder and
virgus put away the skyn of the haddok and lay it in a chargiour
and put the covy aboue and serve it. [A Noble Boke off
Cookry (England, 1468)]

Most recipes for fish in civey prominently include onions, but these
two recipes are unusual in that they omit them.

The first word in the *Wagstaff* version ("Ta") is most likely a
copying error.

177. Soupes Chamlayn
There are two versions of this recipe in *Two Fifteenth-Century
Cookery-Books*.

Soppes pour Chamberleyne. Take wyne, Canell, powder ginger,
sugur/ of eche a porcion; And cast all in a Streynour, And
honge hit on a pyn, And late hit ren thorgh a streynour twies
or thries, til hit ren clere; And then take paynmain, And kutte
hit in a maner of Browes, And tost hit, And ley hit in a dissh,
and caste blanche pouder there-on ynogh; And then cast the
same licour vppon the Soppes, and serue hit forthe fore a good
potage.   [Two Fifteenth-Century Cookery-Books (England,
1430)]

xxviij - Soupes Jamberlayne. Take Wyne, Canel, an powder of
Gyngere, an Sugre, an of eche a porcyoun, than take a
straynoure and hange it on a pynne, an caste ale ther-to, an let
renne twyis or thryis throgh, tyl it renne clere; an then take

Paynemaynne an kyt it in maner of brewes, an toste it, an wete
it in the same lycowre, an ley it on a dysshe, an caste blawnche
powder y-now ther-on; an than caste the same lycour vp-on
the same soppys, an serue hem forth in maner of a potage.
[Two Fifteenth-Century Cookery-Books (England, 1430)]

Spiced wine with slices of sugared toast sounds like a rather odd
soup, though with just enough wine to soak the toast it might be a
pleasant sort dessert.

There is also one variant of cameline sauce that has almost the
same ingredients.

Sauce gamelyne. Take faire brede, and kutte it, and take vinegre
and wyne, and stepe the brede therein, and drawe hit thorgh a
streynour with powder of canel, and drawe hit twies or thries
til hit be smoth; and then take pouder of ginger, Sugur, and
pouder of cloues, and cast therto a litul saffron and lete hit be
thik ynogh, and thenne serue hit forthe.   [Two Fifteenth-
Century Cookery-Books (England, 1430)]

This leads me to wonder if the "soupes" recipes had their origin in
a misinterpretation of a camaline sauce recipe.

178. Coddlyng Leng Haddoke & Hake

This recipe is a variation of recipe 112 from *A Noble Boke off
Cookry*. The recipes are the same right up to where it says to serve
with the liver, but then the *Wagstaff* version adds instructions for
saucing the fish.

To dight codlinge hak or haddok draw them at the belly and
cut them outwhart in rond peces and the haddok be large cut
of the hed and mak a large taile and mak the sauce of water
and salt and when it boilethe scome it clene and cast in the
fische and the lever and parsly and let it ly in the sauce till ye
serue it hot and the leuer there with.   [A Noble Boke off
Cookry (England, 1468)]

179. Bace Mylet or Breme
This recipe is a match for recipe 113 from *A Noble Boke off Cookry*.

> To dight bace molet or breme drawe them at the belly and skale them clene and wesche them and mak ye sauce of water and salt and when it boilithe scom it clene and scoche them outwhat the sides and cast them in at the boiling put ther to parsly and saige and serue it. the bace and the molet with guinger. [A Noble Boke off Cookry (England, 1468)]

180. Congur Turbutt Halibut Poyled
A Noble Boke off Cookry has this recipe broken up into three separate recipes, numbered 114, 115, 116.

> To dight congur. turbot or halibut scald your congur but be ware of brekyng then clef the congur hed and cutt the congur a litille befor the naville and lowse the got and tak it out at the throt and the leuer and the gutte and cut it in rond peces and let it be clene shaven that the skyne be not away. [A Noble Boke off Cookry (England, 1468)]

> and draw the turbot by the gille out of the hed and the body out whart [A Noble Boke off Cookry (England, 1468)]

> and chyne a halibut and sethe hym with water and salt and when it boilithe then skeme it and when the congur is enoughe tak it up with a strene and lay it in a vesselle and when the turbot and halibut is enoughe pour out the brothe and put water ther to and tak up the fische and lay it in water and salt and serue it ij or iij peces of congur in a disshe and straw ther on parsly and serue it furthe with venygar and the turbot and halibut serue it with pouder and venygar. [A Noble Boke off Cookry (England, 1468)]

The recipes diverge widely near the end after instructing to put two or three pieces in a dish.

181. Gurnarde or Roch Boyled

This recipe is a match for recipe 117 from *A Noble Boke off Cookry*.

> To boile gurnard or rochet draw a gurnard at the belly and tak out the sound and the resset and slit the pok shave it clene and let it hang by then wesche it and mak the sauce of water and salt and when it boilithe skom it clene and put in the fisshe and when it is sodden tak it up with a scomer and serue it with sauce guinger. [A Noble Boke off Cookry (England, 1468)]

There also appears to be a related recipe in Two Fifteenth-Century Cookery-Books.

> Gurnard rosted or boyled. Take a Gurnard, and drawe him in the bely and saue the powche with-yn hole; and make sauce of water and salt; And whan hit bigynneth to boile, skeme it clene, And cast the Gurnard thereto, And seth him, and sauce/ to him is sauce of ginger, or vergyussauce, and serue him colde. [Two Fifteenth-Century Cookery-Books (England, 1430)]

182. Playce Solys and Flounderres Boyled

Recipe 118 from *A Noble Boke off Cookry* appears to be a truncated version of this recipe.

> To boile place or flounders tak a place and draw hym under the vyn and draw a flounder and stoche hym outwhart across on the whit side wesche hym and boile hem with water and salt cast ther to parsley and sethe them and serue them with the brothe. [A Noble Boke off Cookry (England, 1468)]

There also appears to be a related recipe in *Two Fifteenth-Century Cookery-Books*.

> ffloundres boiled. Take floundres, and drawe hem in the side by the hede, and seth (Note: Douce MS. scocch) hem, and make sauce of water and salt, and a good quantite of ale; And whan hit biginneth to boile, skeme it, and caste hem there-to; And late hem sethe, and serue hem forth hote; and no sauce

but salt, or as a man luste. [Two Fifteenth-Century Cookery-Books (England, 1430)]

183. Welkes Boyled
This recipe is a match for recipe 119 from *A Noble Boke off Cookry*.

> To boile welks put them in a pot with water so they may flot then set them on the fyer and let them stond longe or they sethe then tak them out of the water and tak out the fisshe with a prik and put away the hulles then wesche them well with watire and salt ij or iij tymes then lay them in clene water till ye serue them with grene parsly. [A Noble Boke off Cookry (England, 1468)]

There is another version of the same recipe in *Two Fifteenth-Century Cookery-Books*.

> Welkes boyled. Take welkes, and caste hem in colde water, And lete hem boyle but a litull; And caste hem oute of the vessell, And pike hem oute of the shell, and pike awey the horn of hem, and wassh hem and rubbe hem well in colde water and salt, in two or thre waters; And serue hem colde, And caste vppon hem leves of parcelly ywet in vinegre, And sauce to hem is vynegre. [Two Fifteenth-Century Cookery-Books (England, 1430)]

184. Perch Boyled
This recipe is a match for recipe 120 from *A Noble Boke off Cookry*.

> To boylle a perche draw hym at the gills and let the belly be hole and mak a stiff sauce of water and salt and ale and when it boilithe cast in the perche and let it sethe and scrape of the skyne and lay it in a disshe and let the hed and the taile be on straw on padley and serue it with venyger. [A Noble Boke off Cookry (England, 1468)]

There is another version of the same recipe in *Two Fifteenth-Century Cookery-Books*.

Perche boiled. Take a perche, and drawe him in the throte, and make to him sauce of water and salt; And whan hit bigynneth to boile, skeme hit and caste the perche there-in, and seth him; and take him vppe, and pul him, and serue him forth colde, and cast vppon him foiles of parcelly. and the sauce is vinegre or vergeous. [Two Fifteenth-Century Cookery-Books (England, 1430)]

185. Fresch Makrell Boyled

This recipe is a match for recipe 121 from *A Noble Boke off Cookry*.

To dight a freche makerelle tak and draw a makerelle at the gil and let the belly be hole and wesche hym and mak the sauce of water and salt and when it boilithe cast in mynt and parsly and put in the fisshe and serue it furthe with sorell sauce. [A Noble Boke off Cookry (England, 1468)]

186. Shrympys Boyled

There is a related recipe in *Two Fifteenth-Century Cookery-Books*.

Shrympes. Take Shrympes, and seth hem in water and a litull salt, and lete hem boile ones or a litull more. And serue hem forthe colde; And no maner sauce but vinegre. [Two Fifteenth-Century Cookery-Books (England, 1430)]

Maybe it is due to boiled shrimp being such an easy dish to make, but I'm surprised there aren't more of such recipes in contemporary sources.

187. Soupys yn Dorye

This recipe is a match for recipe 122 from *A Noble Boke off Cookry*.

To mak soupes in doce grinde blanched almondes and serup them up with water into a faire mylke and draw it into a pot through a strener put ther to sugur saffron and salt set it on the fyere and stirr it welle when it boilith do it to a litill wyn and tak it from the fyere and stirr it well for qualinge then cutt whit bred in shyues and toist it on a gredirne that it be browne then put them in wyne and lay them on the gredirne agayne and lay the toistes iij or iiij in a disshe and put on the mylk and serue it. [A Noble Boke off Cookry (England, 1468)]

There are many versions of Soups Dorre in other sources, suggesting that it was a popular dish. *Two Fifteenth-Century Cookery-Books* has two notably different versions.

Soppes Dorre. Take rawe Almondes, And grynde hem in A morter, And temper hem with wyn and drawe hem thorgh a streynour; And lete hem boyle, And cast there-to Saffron, Sugur, and salt; And then take a paynmain, And kut him and tost him, And wete him in wyne, And ley hem in a dissh, and caste the siryppe thereon, and make a dregge of pouder ginger, sugur, Canell, Clowes, and maces, And cast thereon; And whan hit is I-Dressed, serue it forth fore a good potage. [Two Fifteenth-Century Cookery-Books (England, 1430)]

Soupes dorroy. Shere Oynonys, an frye hem in oyle; thanne take Wyne, an boyle with Oynonys, toste whyte Brede an do on a dysshe, an caste ther-on gode Almaunde Mylke, and temper it wyth wyne: thanne do the dorry a-bowte, an messe it forth. [Two Fifteenth-Century Cookery-Books (England, 1430)]

Both of these types are also present in Forme of Cury, showing that the recipe calling for onions isn't a fluke.

Sowpes Dorry. XX.IIII. II. Take Almaundes brayed, drawe hem up with wyne. ooile it, cast þeruppon safroun and salt, take brede itosted in wyne. lay þerof a leyne and anoþer of þe sewe and alle togydre. florish it with sugur powdour gyngur and serue it forth. [Forme of Cury (England, 1390)]

FOR TO MAKE SOWPYS DORRY. Nym onyons and mynce hem smale and fry hem in oyl dolyf Nym wyn and boyle yt wyth the onyouns roste wyte bred and do yt in dischis and god Almande mylk also and do ther'above and serve yt forthe. [Forme of Cury (England, 1390)]

188. Hote Mylke of Almoundys
This recipe is a match for recipe 123 from *A Noble Boke off Cookry*.

To mak hot mylk of almonds tak blanched almonds and grind
them and draw them with faire water and sugur or Hony
clarified then salt it and boile it and serue it furthe hoot and
toisted bred ther in.   [A Noble Boke off Cookry (England,
1468)]

189. Cold Mylke of Almondys
This recipe is a match for recipe 124 from *A Noble Boke off Cookry*.

To mak cold mylk of almondes put fair water in a pot with
sugur or hony clarified so that it be douce then salt it and set it
on the fyere and when it is at boilling scom it and let it boile
awhile then tak it from the fyere and let it kele then blanche
youre almondes and grind them and temper them with the
same water in to a good thik mylk and put it to wyne that it
may haue a good flavour ther of and serue it then cut bred and
toist it and baist it and toist it again that it be hard and serue
them in one disshe and the mylk in an other disshe. [A Noble
Boke off Cookry (England, 1468)]

Of the 189 recipes in the *Wagstaff Miscellany*, 132 have a corresponding recipe in *A Noble Boke off Cookry*. Additionally, there are long sequences of recipes that appear in both sources in the same order. While this suggests the two cookbooks are closely related, I have not been able to determine if one was a source for the other, or if both drew from a common source.

The table below lists all of the *Wagstaff* recipes along with the corresponding recipe from *Noble* when possible.

1. (untitled recipe) .... 142. Wortis
2. For to make canabenes .... 143. Canebyns
3. Canabens .... 144. Another canebyns
4. Canabens With Bacone .... 145. Canebyns with bacon
5. Butturde Wortys .... 146. Buttered worts
6. Cabogys .... 147. Cabage wortis
7. Hare or goose .... 148. Haire or goose
8. Joutys .... []
9. Lentyn foyles .... []
10. Longe wortys .... []
11. Blaunche porre .... []
12. Pome perre .... []
13. Gingaudre .... []
14. Eles yne sorre .... []
15. Pykes or elys .... 149. Pik and eles
16. Frumente yne lentyne .... 150. Furmente with porpas
17. Pylets yne sarcene .... []
18. Jussalle .... 151. Jusselle
19. leche lardys .... []
20. umbelys of a dere .... []
21. Grewel enforsede .... 153. Gruelle enforced
22. Chaudone of Salmone .... 154. Chaudron for samon
23. Cokkes of kellynge .... 155. Codling or kelyng
24. Felets yne galentyne .... 157. Felettes in galentyne
25. Leche provene .... []
26. Numbelys of purpas .... 158. Nombles of porpas
27. Purpayse .... []
28. Purpayse or Venysone .... []
29. Hare yne cyve .... []
30. Hare yne papalde .... 223. Haires in pardolos

31. Hare yne talbut .... [ ]
32. Conynggez in gravee .... 133. Cony or malard in covy
33. Conynggez in Cyve .... [ ]
34. Conyngges yne brothe .... [ ]
35. Oysters in grave .... [ ]
36. Oystres in Cyve .... [ ]
37. Chikens in gretney .... 8. Chekins in kirtin
38. Creteyney .... [ ]
39. Capons yne conceps .... 231. Capon in couns
40. Chikens yne caudelle .... 226. Chekins in cawdelle
41. Soupes .... [ ]
42. Chaudone of Veel .... [ ]
43. Chaudone of Pigges fete .... 159. Chaudron of piggs feet
44. Bonse desyre .... 26. Bland sorre
45. Bruet of lumbardy .... 160. Bruet of Lombardy
46. Bruet of Almayne .... [ ]
47. Bruet of Spayne .... 161. Bruet of Spayne
48. Bruet roos .... 162. Bruet rosse
49. Chikens yne bruet .... [ ]
50. Stewe lumbarde .... 163 & 164 (merged)
51. Stewy colops .... 165. Stewed colopes
52. Bruet tuskyne .... 166. Busbayne
53. Bruet sarcenes .... [ ]
54. Bruet of kedes .... 167. Bruet of kiddes
55. Blaunche Bruet .... 168. Blanche Bruet
56. Sauce sarcenes........................ 169. Sauce sairsnet
57. Veel in bucnade .... [ ]
58. Pynonade .... [ ]
59. Kyd stewyde .... 170. To stewe a kid
60. Stewyde pertryche .... 171. Pertuche stewed
61. A losede beef .... 172. A lowsid bef
62. Pyke in sauce .... 173. To dight a pik
63. Turbut rostyde .... 174. To dight turbot
64. Salmone rostyde .... 175. Samon rost
65. Brawne in confyte .... 176. Breme in comfet
66. Leche Lumbarde .... [ ]
67. Tayle .... [ ]
68. Blaunche de sorre .... [ ]
69. Blaw maungere .... [ ]
70. Blaunche Doucet .... [ ]

71. Chikeney .... [ ]
72. Blanke desyre .... [ ]
73. Dage .... [ ]
74. Sypers .... [ ]
75. Floreye .... 197. Rose
76. Creme boyled .... 17. Creme buile
77. Lyed mylke .... 179. Alayd mylk
78. Moretruys of wresch fysch ... [ ]
79. Mortruys of flesch .... [ ]
80. Blaunch mortruys of fisch .... [ ]
81. Blaunch mortruys .... [ ]
82. Paynd foundow .... [ ]
83. Caudell .... [ ]
84. Caudell fery .... [ ]
85. Charlet.................................. 191. Charlet
86. Perys in confyte .... [ ]
87. Perys in composte................. 180. Peres in composte
88. Perys in Syrup .... [ ]
89. Brawn ryal .... 177. Braun Rialle
90. Brawn ryall .... 33. Braun ryall
91. Betrayn yn lentyn .... 34. Breteyne
92. Betreyn in flesch tyme .... 35. Bretyn in fleshe tym
93. Storgeon for sopers .... 36. Sturgion for sopers
94. Cold lech viaund .... 37. Cold lesche viand
95. Lech lumbard .... 22. Lesk Lombard
96. Cold bruet of rabbets .... 38. Cold bruet for rabettes
97. Dyvers desire .... [ ]
98. Viaund ryall .... [ ]
99. Mawmene ryall .... [ ]
100. Gely on fysch days .... [ ]
101. Cristell gely .... 39. Cristalle Gilly
102. Gely of flesch .... 40. Gilly of fleshe
103. Creme of almondys .... 41. Creme of almonds
104. Hages of Almayne .... 42. Hagges of Almayne
105. Quystes .... 43. Quystis
106. Vontes .... 44. Votose
107. Bastons .... 45. Rostand
108. Samatays .... 46. Samartard
109. Long Fryturys .... 47. Longe fritturs
110. Payn purdyeu .... 48. Payn pardieu

111. Ffelets of porke yn doryd..... 49. Pestelles of pork
112. Hattes .... 50. Hattes in flesshe tyme
113. (Hattes) In lentyn .... 51. Hattes in lent
114. Sauce Madam .... 52. Sauce Madame
115. Sauce camelyn .... 53. Sauce Camelyne
116. Chaudon of Swan .... 54. Chandron for swannes
117. Wellyd pepyr .... 57. Wellid peper
118. Fresch lamprey bakyn .... 55. To bak a freche lampry
119. Tartes of Flesch .... 58. Tartes of fleshe
120. Tartelets .... 59. To mak tartalettes
121. Bakyn purpays .... 60. To bak porpas
122. Pyes of flesch .... 61. Pyes of flesche
123. Crustad lumbard .... 62. Custad Lombard
124. Chauet of Beef .... 64. Chewettes of beef
125. Chauet Ryall .... 66. Chewettes rialle
126. Bakyn chikenes .... 65. To bak chekyns
127. Chauet yn fysch dayes .... 67. Chewettes on fische dais
128. Darrolete .... 68. Dariolites
129. Prineroll at pasche .... 69. Prymerolle in pasthe
130. To Make a Possote .... 70. To mak a posthot
131. Pyes of Pares .... 72. Pyes of Pairis
132. Brinddy .... 71. Breney
133. Losyngys opyn .... 73. Lossenges fried in lent
134. Harbelet opyn .... 74. Hairblad opyne
135. Leche fryed .... 75. Lesche freey
136. Bakyn Mete on Fisch Dayes 76. Bak metes on fysshe days
137. A Bakyn Mete Opyn .... [ ]
138. A Colde Bakyn Mete .... [ ]
139. Caudell of Almondys .... [ ]
140. Sle Aner of Foules .... 77. To Sley a Swan
141. Crane Rostyd .... 81. A Crayne
142. Fesaunte Rostyd .... 78. A Fessand
143. Pertrich Rostyd .... 79. A Pertuehe
144. Quayle Rostyd .... 80. A quayle
145. Heyron Rostyd .... 82. A heron
146. Bytare Rostyd .... 83. A Bittur
147. Egrett Rostyd .... 84. An Egret
148. Curlew Rostyd .... 85. A Curlew
149. Grew Rostyd .... 86. A Brewe
150. Conynggys Rostyd .... 87. A Conye

GLOSSARY

brawn (also: braun, braune) - Flesh. The term is typically only applied to meat.

canell (also: canel, canelle) - Cassia (*Cinnamomum cassia* - Sold as "cinnamon" in the United States). Possibly cinnamon (*Cinnamomum zeylenicum*) as well.

caudle (also: caudell) - A smooth, thick soup or beverage, usually made with eggs.

chargaunt (also: chargeaunt) - Very thick. Chargeant seems to be somewhere between "thick" and "stonding" in consistency.

chewett (also: chauet) -

civey (also: cyve) - Meat gravy, typically made with onions.

coles (also: caules, caulys) - Any one of a number of leafy vegetables, usually a variant of cabbage (*Brassica oleracea*).

colops - Slices of meat (i.e. "scallops").

culpon - Slices or shreds of meat.

dight (also: dyght, dyghte) - To carve. The term is typically used for game birds.

egyr - Sour, from the French "aigre"

eiren (also: ayron, eyren, eyroun, eyryn) - Eggs, from the German "eier".farced: stuffed

fee - Liver.

gleyre - Egg white

grue - A craine (*Grus grus*).

groin (also: groyne) - A pig's snout, from middle French.

hastlet - A fillet.

humbles (also numbelys, umbelys) -

joutes (also joutys, jowtys) - Herbs cooked in broth or almond milk.

keeling (also keeling, kelynge) - A type of cod.

leche (also lesh, lesche) - To slice, or a slice.

lyre - The muscle of the thigh. Also, a mix of bread and a liquid, usually broth or wine, used as a sauce (a corruption of "liquor").

meddle - To mix.

mortrues - A dish of pounded or ground meat.

numbles (also nombles, nomblys, humbles) - Entrails, usually the kidneys.

okekornes – Acorns (lit. "oak cornes").

osey - A type of sweet wine, possibly from France or Portugal.

payndemayne (also pain demesne) - Fine, white bread.

quall (also quayle, quail) - To curdle or coagulate.

quyste - A wood pigeon.

sarcelle (also sorcell) - The common teal (*Anas crecca*)

saunders - Powdered red sandalwood (*Pterocarpus santalinus*), used as a colorant.

seethe - Boil, boiled.

stondyng - Extremely thick, like thick oatmeal (lit. "standing").

swyng - To beat or whip.

tharmes – Entrails.

trene - Wooden (lit. "tree-en").

trie - To separate or tease apart.

turnsol - A number of plants of the genus Heliotropium, used to produce red, purple, or blue colors.

umbles - See "numbles"

wortes - Edible green plants and leafy herbs.

yarmazs - Entrails, a corruption of "tharmes".

BIBLIOGRAPHY

Austin, Thomas. *Two Fifteenth-century Cookery-books. Harleian Ms. 279 (ab. 1430), & Harl. Ms. 4016 (ab. 1450), with Extracts from Ashmole Ms. 1429, Laud Ms. 553, & Douce Ms. 55.* London: Pub. for the Early English Text Society by N. Trübner &, 1888. Print.

Chiquart, Terence Scully, and Maurice Casanova. *Du Fait De Cuisine.* Sion: Bibliothèque Et Des Archives Cantonales Du Valais, 1985. Print.

Cotgrave, R. *A Dictionarie of the French and English Tongues.* London: Printed by A. Islip, 1611. Print.

Matterer, James. "Gentyll manly Cokere" (MS Pepys 1047). Gode Cookery, n.d. Web. 28 May 2013.

Mayhew, Anthony Lawson., and Walter William. Skeat. *A Concise Dictionary of Middle English: From A.D. 1150 to 1580.* Oxford: At the Clarendon, 1888. Print.

Morris, Richard. *Liber Cure Cocorum.* Berlin: Published for the Philological Society by A. Asher &, 1862. Print.

Myers, Daniel. "Enseignements." *Enseignements.* Medieval Cookery, 2005. Web. 28 May 2013.

Napier, Robina. *A Noble Boke off Cookry*. Lond.: Elliot Stock, 1882. Print.

Pegge, Samuel, Richard, and Gustavus Brander. *The Forme of Cury: A Roll of Ancient English Cookery, Compiled, about A.D. 1390, by the Master-cooks of ... Richard II ... and Now in the Possession of Gustavus Brander, Esq.* London: J. Nichols, 1780. Print.

Waks, Mark, and Jane Waks. "A Book of Cookrye." *A Book of Cookrye*. A Book of Cookrye, n.d. Web. 18 Mar. 2014.

Warner, Richard. *Antiquitates Culinariae = or Curious Tracts Relating to the Culinary Affairs of the Old English*. N.p.: Printed for R. Blamire, 1791. Print.